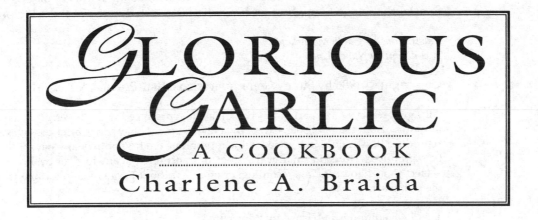

GLORIOUS GARLIC
A COOKBOOK
Charlene A. Braida

WINGS BOOKS

New York • Avenel, New Jersey

This book is dedicated to my parents, Theresa and Charles Braida.
My mother in particular taught me that cooking is an adventure in textures,
colors, and tastes, and her inspiration and assistance made this book possible.
Special thanks go to my brother Jim, who taste-tested many of these recipes.

Illustrations by Cindy McFarland
Text design by Nancy Lamb

This 1995 edition is published by Wings Books,
distributed by Random House Value Publishing, Inc.,
40 Engelhard Avenue, Avenel, New Jersey 07001,
by arrangement with Storey Communications, Inc.

Random House
New York • Toronto • London • Sydney • Auckland

Printed and bound in the United States of America

Library of Congress Cataloging–in–Publication Data

Braida, Charlene A., 1952–
    Glorious garlic : a cookbook / by Charlene A. Braida.
            p.   cm.
    Originally published: Pownal, VT : Storey Communications, c1986.
    Includes index.
    ISBN 0–517–14660–6 (hc)
    1. Cookery (Garlic) 2. Garlic. I. Title.
TX819.G3B73   1995   95–20043
641.6′526—dc20   CIP

8 7 6 5 4 3 2 1

Table of Contents

———Introduction

"Each clove of garlic has a sacred power . . ."

FLOWERS AND FLOWER LORE
Reverend Hilderic Friend, 1891

Garlic Fever

One of my earliest memories is of awakening to the redolent aroma of garlic sautéing in olive oil, as my mother began her weekly ritual of preparing tomato sauce for our traditional Sunday pasta dinner. That garlicky fragrance still symbolizes to me the essence of a good meal; it stimulates the taste buds and promises something delicious to come.

To sit down to a meal cooked with garlic is not only to taste something delicious, but also to do something good for yourself—because garlic's powers are many, not just in myth but in fact.

Garlic has been esteemed since ancient times as an aphrodisiac, an amulet, and a panacea. When it comes to cooking, however, garlic earns its highest praise. It imparts to foods a certain accent, emphasis, and zip. It makes an ordinary dish exciting. The taste of this delightful herb can range from pungent to delicate and from sharp to almost sweet and nutty. Its versatility makes it an excellent accompaniment to vegetables, meat, poultry, fish, and pasta. The recipes assembled here illustrate the varied uses of garlic and they provide a repertoire of garlic-laced foods that will make your taste buds tingle with excitement.

Historically, garlic has received mixed reviews— heralded by some, scorned by others, sometimes in favor and fashion with the ruling classes and other times deemed fit only for the peasantry. Even when garlic has received the gastronomical appreciation it deserves, claims of its medicinal powers and magical charms have been greeted with skepticism. This controversial history only adds to the allure of garlic.

Today, garlic is enjoying a well-deserved recognition. It has become indispensable in everyday cooking as well as in *haute cuisine*, sparking a dramatic increase in garlic consumption in the last decade.

Despite this increased interest in cooking with garlic, however, some people have yet to discover the varied charms of this wondrous herb. I hope that through the recipes and information contained in this cookbook you will discover more of the myriad possibilities of garlic.

My Garlic Roots

The idea for this cookbook began with the realization that my family has been blessed with some pretty talented cooks, namely my mother, Theresa, and my two grandmothers. Several of my grandmothers' recipes are included here, but my mother is the primary source of recipes for this book. The ethnic orientation of her cooking is Italian, primarily Neapolitan. As a first-generation Italian-American, she acquired some of her culinary skills while growing up on a farm in southern New Jersey. When she married my father, she increased her repertoire by learning to cook the Northern Italian dishes his mother prepared.

There is a definite difference in the cooking of the various regions of Italy. (The parochialism of each region is strikingly evident in the wide array of Italian dialects as well, which vary to such an extent that communication among different regional groups is often difficult.) In general, Northern Italian dishes feature cream sauces, polenta (cornmeal), and the frequent use of cinnamon and allspice. Neapolitan cuisine, on the other hand, features tomato sauces and pastas, a preference for olive oil, and perhaps slightly more garlic. For my mother and for Italian cooks in general, garlic is an integral flavoring, so much so that the preparation of almost every meal begins with the sautéing of garlic in vegetable or olive oil.

To insure that this tradition of cooking would continue through another generation, I decided to write down some of my favorite family recipes. I spent months following my mother around her kitchen, learning and observing her cooking methods and habits and interrupting her progress as I converted pinches or dashes or handfuls of ingredients into standardized units of measurement. With extensive cooking experience, such as my mother has, exactitude often gives way to a certain intuition about how a dish should be prepared. In that sense, consider these recipes a starting point for experimentation.

Other Garlicky Cuisines

Italian food is not the only cuisine that favors the abundant use of garlic. One of the most commonly used seasonings in Spanish cooking, garlic is found in such dishes as *gazpacho*, a cold vegetable soup. The French are famous for their sauces, and garlic is used in many of them, including *aïoli*, a classic garlic-flavored mayonnaise. French cooks also add handfuls of whole garlic cloves to soup stocks and to chicken for roasting.

Along with eggplant, lamb, yogurt, and tomato, garlic is one of the staples of Middle-Eastern cuisine. *Hummus*, a dish made of chick peas and garlic, is a popular Middle-Eastern food. In Israel, a different mixture of chick peas and garlic is shaped into balls and deep fried, to create *falafel*.

In Chinese cooking there are a number of distinctive cooking styles, at least two of which, Hunan and Szechuan, include the use of garlic. A good deal of garlic is used in Szechuan food, particularly, which is generally hot and spicy.

Medicinal Benefits

Throughout history, garlic has been revered for its magical healing powers. The *Ebers Papyrus*, an early Egyptian medical treatise dating to about 1500 B.C., mentions it as a cure for numerous ailments, from headaches and tumors to heart problems. It was so valuable that fifteen pounds of bulbs once bought an Egyptian slave. Hippocrates recognized its effectiveness in the treatment of infections, and Discordes, a Greek physician who administered to the Roman army in the first century B.C., prescribed it for intestinal maladies and as a vermifuge. Galen, a Roman physician in the second century A.D., believed that garlic was a cure-all for numerous afflictions and, in particular, an antidote for certain poisons. Pliny the Elder, the Roman naturalist, advocated its use as a remedy for sixty-one health problems, including toothaches, ulcers, and asthma; and the prophet Mohammed recommended it for the treatment of snake and scorpion bites.

Medicine men of certain American Indian tribes used to administer garlic as a treatment for bronchitis and asthma. In addition, they are known to have prescribed garlic tea as a vermifuge and a garlic-based syrup as a cure for headaches.

Chinese herbalists reportedly have viewed garlic as a broad-spectrum antibiotic, effective in the treatment of respiratory ailments. They have recommended garlic tea for persistent coughs and a syrupy mixture of garlic broth, honey, and vinegar as an expectorant for chronic bronchitis. Among the Chinese, garlic also is reputed to reduce high blood pressure.

Scientific studies support many of these claims. In the mid-1800s, Louis Pasteur confirmed that the allicin in garlic has antibacterial properties, and during both World Wars garlic was administered to prevent gangrene.

Garlic is good news for persons with heart disease, whose arteries have been narrowed by the accumulation of fatty deposits. Occasionally, at these fatty deposit sites, unwanted clots break away, travel to the heart, and cause a heart attack. In the 1970s, Dr. Arun Bordia and his colleagues at the Tagore Medical College in India demonstrated that garlic helps break down a substance called fibrin, an essential component of blood clots. Increased fibrin breakdown can therefore be life-saving. Researchers at the Wistar Institute of Anatomy and Biology in Philadelphia, meanwhile, have reported that garlic oil inhibits formation of fatty deposits in the arteries of rabbits.

Dr. Bordia and his colleagues have also demonstrated that garlic helps reduce cholesterol. And if that's not enough, recent reports out of China disclose that cancer researchers in that country believe they have proven garlic to be effective in blocking formation of a certain carcinogen, nitrosamine.

Incidentally, garlic is truly beneficial from head to toe: recent experiments have revealed that garlic juice inhibits the growth of certain fungi that cause ringworm and athlete's foot.

Special Powers

Garlic's aphrodisiac qualities have been extolled through the centuries. Wandering Israelites, freed from slavery in Egypt, yearned for garlic, which they characterized as a "hot food" capable of stimulating sexual desire. Ancient Romans revered garlic's aphrodisiacal powers; and Pliny the Elder recommended "love potions" made by mixing garlic and other spices, such as coriander, with wine. In some eastern cultures, garlic is regarded as an arousal agent, having longer-lasting effects than other herbal aphrodisiacs due to its reputed ability to revitalize the whole body through stimulation of gastric juices and hormonal secretions. Aristophanes, the Greek playwright, claimed that garlic could restore one's masculine vigor, and Henry IV of France reportedly consumed garlic before venturing on each of his amorous adventures.

Besides the power of love, garlic is believed by some to possess magical powers. Odysseus protected himself against the sorcery of Circe with a species of wild garlic. The ancient Greeks placed piles of garlic at crossroads as offerings to Hecate, the underworld goddess of magic and charms. Greek peasant women even today guard against the malice and envy of capricious supernatural beings called Nereids by hanging bunches of garlic at the entrances to their homes upon the occasions of marriage and childbirth. In Italy and Greece, it is used as protection against the "evil eye," and in India, it is worn for protection against demons.

In many cultures garlic's power extended even to the after-life. Six cloves of garlic were found in King Tut's tomb, and in pre-dynastic Egyptian cemeteries, clay models of garlic bulbs have been found buried along with the dead. In Central and Eastern Europe, garlic was placed in the coffins of suspected vampires to keep them from rising from the dead.

Botanical History

Allium sativum, as garlic is known botanically, is a member of the lily family to which leeks, onions, and shallots also belong. Although authorities differ, garlic is generally regarded as being indigenous to Central Asia. It was cultivated in the Mediterranean region from at least early Egyptian times and was mentioned as a food staple in the writings of the Sumerians as early as 3,000 B.C. It was probably brought to America by the Europeans, although a variety of wild garlic was eaten as a vegetable by pre-Columbian Indians prior to any European exploration of the New World.

As garlic grows, it sends up a green stalk about 2 feet tall, while a bulb, comprised of ten or more sections called cloves, develops underground. It grows best in light, sandy soil in regions that, like California, can boast of sunny days and long growing seasons. France, Italy, and Mexico also produce garlic as a cash crop.

Varieties

Numerous varieties of garlic are grown throughout the world. The color of the skin ranges from white to dark purple and clove shape varies from long and slender to short and fat. In California, the two most popular varieties are known as California Early White and Late White garlic. Early garlic is planted in September and matures about a month ahead of late garlic. It is larger and slightly flatter in shape, and its parchment-like skin is off-white in color. Late garlic is the preferred variety because of its long shelf life, usually more than six months (at least two months longer than the early variety). The outer sheathing of late garlic is white, and the skin of the cloves varies from light pink to red.

Another variety of interest is elephant garlic, so named because of its size. The plants can grow as high as 3 feet, and two garlic bulbs can weigh a pound. The flavor and aroma of elephant garlic are more subtle than some other varieties.

Buying Garlic

There is only one way to buy garlic, and that's fresh—anything else is second rate. It is available in the processed forms of dehydrated garlic powder and garlic salt, but neither the flavor nor the aroma of these products can compare with that of fresh.

Choose firm bulbs without cuts, bruises, or damaged skins. The size of the cloves is unimportant. If the cloves are smaller than average, just use two cloves for every one the recipe requires. Garlic is also available minced and packed in vegetable oil; it should be refrigerated after opening.

Garlic butter (butter mixed with crushed garlic), garlic oil (oil flavored with crushed garlic), and garlic-flavored vinegar are also available commercially or can be easily prepared at home.

Cooking with Garlic

The flavor garlic imparts depends on the amount, the variety, and, most important, the manner in which it is prepared. Raw garlic is stronger in taste and smell than cooked garlic, and, for that reason, a little will go a long way. For just a hint of garlic in a tossed green salad, rub a raw clove around the inside of a wooden bowl before filling it with salad ingredients.

The longer garlic is cooked, the more delicate its flavor. Heat destroys the chemical substance allicin, which is responsible for the herb's characteristic flavor and aroma. When whole garlic cloves are baked for a long time, they develop a sweet and nutty flavor; therefore, a baked-chicken recipe requiring twenty cloves of garlic is not as outrageous as it might seem. Large wedges of garlic can be embedded in venison, lamb, and pork roasts to contribute a delicate flavor to these meats as they slowly cook. Sliced or chopped garlic lightly sautéed in oil can be added to virtually any cooked vegetable. Be careful never to allow sautéed garlic to become dark brown or to burn, because it will taste bitter. It is best to discard both the burned garlic and the oil in which it was sautéed and start over again with fresh ingredients.

The more garlic is crushed or cut, the stronger its flavor becomes. The process of cutting or crushing severs the cell membranes, allowing a certain amino acid to react with a specific enzyme to create the substance allicin. To crush garlic, either use a garlic press or place a clove on a cutting board and press down on it with a heavy knife handle or rolling pin. To mince garlic, I like to use a very sharp paring knife with a small, slender blade.

Ordinarily, garlic is not difficult to peel. Just cut across both ends of the clove, and the skin should fall off when prodded with a knife blade. Occasionally, the skin may be very tight; if it resists peeling, press the clove with the flat of a knife blade until the skin cracks. It will then come off easily.

Aroma

I may be too much of a garlic fan to consider its bouquet anything less than marvelous. Fear of having garlic on one's breath, however, can dampen enjoyment of this flavorful herb. "Garlic breath" is usually associated with eating the bulb raw. One simple antidote is to chew parsley or any raw vegetable containing chlorophyll, for an instant breath freshener. Green cardamom pods will also do the trick. Another solution is to surround yourself with people who are also eating garlicky foods.

When you prepare garlic for cooking, you will undoubtedly wind up with its tenacious odor on your hands. To eliminate it, wash your hands in warm sudsy water and rub them with fresh parsley or lemon juice.

Home-Grown Garlic

My father has been growing gorgeous garlic in his New Jersey garden for years. He recommends the following method:

Select an area of your garden that has good drainage. In early September, prepare the ground by cultivating or loosening the soil with hand tools to a depth of 4 to 6 inches and removing any weeds. About the third week in September, plant the garlic by placing individual cloves, with the pointed end up, 1½ to 2 inches deep and 4 to 5 inches apart. Garlic shoots will appear 2 to 3 inches above ground usually in about four weeks, before the cold weather arrives.

Be sure to mulch around the shoots with leaves or hay to protect the plants during the winter. Once cold weather arrives, the garlic will remain dormant until spring. When the frost is out of the ground and the shoots begin to grow again, give the plants a side dressing of fertilizer to encourage their growth. (Place the fertilizer 4 to 6 inches on either side of the bulbs to avoid "burning" the bulb.) Irrigate and cultivate the garlic periodically. When the plants have matured and the shoots are about to turn yellow (in early June), stop watering and allow the ground to dry out. When the top growth is brittle and the ground is dry, it is time to harvest.

Choose a sunny, dry day for harvesting. Undercut the garlic and loosen the soil to remove the bulbs. Be careful when pulling the bulbs that you do not damage the skin or pulp. Allow the garlic to dry out on top of the ground as you harvest it. Rub off the loose dirt, then transfer the bulbs to a wood slatted or wire rack that allows for good air circulation. The garlic should be placed in the sun during the day and protected from dampness and humidity at night by being moved to a warm, dry place such as a shed or garage. Cure (dry) for several weeks.

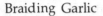
Braiding Garlic

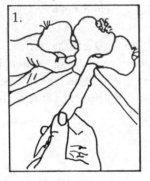

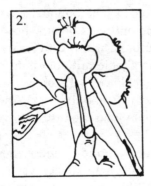

3.

The bulbs are sufficiently cured when the paper-like skin covering the bulbs and the cloves is very dry and brittle; the garlic feels very hard to the touch; the root end is dried out; and the cloves can be separated easily without being damaged. The cured garlic should be stored in a dry, well-ventilated area. Select a number of the best-looking bulbs and separate them into cloves for planting next year's crop. Use just the outer cloves for seed.

Braid garlic before tops are completely dry. Light reinforcing wire is usually required for a long-lasting braid.

These guidelines for growing garlic are based on weather conditions in the mid-Atlantic states. Some variations may be necessary for other parts of the country.

Storage of Garlic

For longest at-home storage, garlic should be kept in a dry, airy spot. Avoid placing it in plastic bags or covered containers, or in any location that does not allow for good circulation of air. Fresh garlic should not be refrigerated. Do not store garlic near other foods like potatoes or apples that might absorb its flavor.

Look for a "garlic cellar"—a small clay pot with a lid and holes in it. Keep in a well-ventilated spot.

Clues to this Cookbook

I almost always use large cloves of garlic, unless they are going to remain uncooked—raw garlic is considerably more potent than cooked. If a smaller size is recommended, the recipe will say so.

When I use the term "sauté," I mean to cook in a light oil or butter base at a controlled heat. When sautéing garlic with onions, in particular, the idea is to control the heat so that the garlic doesn't burn while the onions, which take longer to cook, are softening. The garlic is there to flavor the onions and the oil.

It is difficult to be precise about the amount of oil needed for different cooking tasks. Some vegetables, for example, absorb more than others. It also depends on the size of the pan you are using. Generally, unless you are deep-frying, you need only a thin coat of oil on the surface of the pan. In some of my recipes, although cooking oil is used at several points in the preparation, I have given only the total amount needed in the ingredients list. The recipe instructions will tell you when and how much oil to use at each step.

I add a small amount of salt to the cooking water for vegetables and pasta and have included this instruction in my recipes. If you prefer to eliminate that use of salt, however, you won't harm the recipe.

Side-dish Vegetables

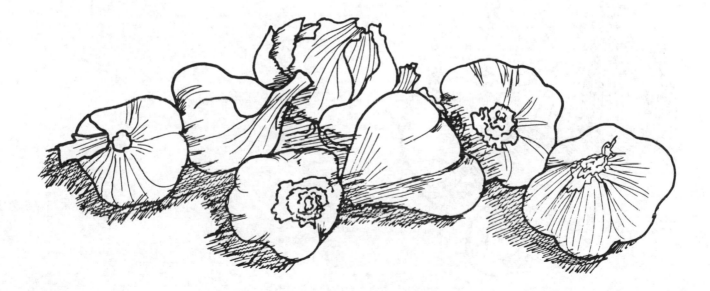

*"Wel loved he garleek, onyons, and eek lekes,
And for to drynken strong wyn, reed as blood."*

THE CANTERBURY TALES
Chaucer

Until you have tasted fresh vegetables cooked with garlic, you haven't experienced their most succulent flavor. Garlic sautéed with spinach or kale transforms these ordinary greens into greens *extraordinaire*. Garlic adds zest to asparagus, broccoli, tomatoes, and a variety of other vegetables.

Another prerequisite for great vegetable cookery is to use the freshest vegetables available. Little can compare with the taste of sweet corn cooked just minutes after being harvested, or the delectable flavor of vine-ripened tomatoes, or the aroma of freshly picked basil. Eating is a sensual experience, and fresh vegetables help to set the proper mood for visual, textural, and tasteful delights, enhanced even further by the accents of garlic in these recipes.

Home gardeners have an obvious advantage in obtaining fresh vegetables, but non-gardeners can come close by familiarizing themselves with the availability of each vegetable in their locality throughout the year.

Living in rural southern New Jersey affords me easy access to a variety of fresh vegetables from March to early October. Vineland, my hometown, is in Cumberland County, which takes pride in its farming families and the large percentage of land under cultivation. Vineland was the site of the 1985 Jersey Fresh Festival—a program sponsored by the New Jersey Department of Agriculture as a promotional vehicle for New Jersey fruits and vegetables. This event highlighted the agricultural strengths of New Jersey—fertile soil, temperate climate, and convenient access to large population centers.

Once you have procured some lovely fresh vegetables, keep in mind the following recommended cooking procedures: To boil vegetables, use the smallest amount of water possible (except with beets or potatoes); bring the water to a rapid boil before adding the vegetables; and cover the pot with a lid to minimize the loss of nutrients and flavors while cooking. To reduce the loss of nutrients and flavors even further, vegetables can be steamed or sautéed.

Everyone develops his or her own preference as to proper cooking times for vegetables. From a nutritional perspective, the shorter the cooking time, the more vitamins and minerals retained. However, you should tailor the cooking times in these recipes to achieve the degree of doneness that you and your dinner guests prefer.

dandelion salad

SERVES 2
PREPARATION TIME:
20 MINUTES

½ pound dandelion leaves
2 hard-boiled eggs, sliced
5 tablespoons vegetable oil
1½ teaspoons vinegar
1 garlic clove, finely chopped
½ teaspoon salt
⅛ teaspoon pepper

Besides being flavorful, dandelions contain high amounts of vitamins A and C, as well as iron. Although some people eat the dandelion found growing in lawns and fields in early spring, I recommend purchasing this green leafy vegetable at local farmers' markets. It will probably be of better quality. Dandelions are grown commercially in New Jersey, where my hometown is the self-proclaimed dandelion capital of the country. (In fact, a former mayor, Patrick Fiorelli, serves an annual dinner featuring dandelions in every course, from appetizers to dessert.) It is best to buy dandelion when it first comes on the market in early spring, since it is then the most tender. The taste is distinctive, somewhat sharper than spinach or collard greens. Try serving this salad with garlic bread.

1. Clean the dandelion by removing the roots and shaking out all the sand. Discard brown or unsightly leaves. Cut into 3-inch segments. Rinse thoroughly in cold water, 4–5 times, being careful to wash away all sand. Drain in a colander and then remove excess water by draining on paper towels.

2. Combine all the ingredients. The volume of the greens will be reduced by about half by the addition of the liquid ingredients. Allow 5–10 minutes for the flavors to mingle before serving.

broccoli salad

SERVES 4–6
PREPARATION TIME:
20–30 MINUTES

Fresh broccoli is abundantly available year round. Choose crisp-looking bluish-green heads with tight buds. For more even cooking, try peeling very thick, tough stalks. Frozen broccoli spears may be used if fresh broccoli is not available.

Be sure to dice the garlic as finely as possible so that its flavor will be evenly distributed in the salad.

2 pounds broccoli
¼–½ cup vegetable oil
2 teaspoons vinegar
dash oregano
1 teaspoon salt
½ teaspoon pepper
1 large garlic clove, finely diced

1. Separate the heads of broccoli into small branchlets, or spears, and remove the excess leaves. Rinse in cold water and drain.

2. In a saucepan, bring 1 cup lightly salted water to a boil. Add the broccoli and cook until tender (about 5 minutes depending on the thickness of the stalks). Do not overcook. Drain the broccoli and place it in a bowl.

3. While the broccoli is still warm, add the oil, vinegar, oregano, salt, pepper, and garlic. Toss the broccoli until well coated with oil, vinegar, and seasonings. Allow the seasonings to mingle for about 10 minutes before serving the salad.

broccoli cheese casserole

SERVES 6
PREPARATION TIME:
60 MINUTES

Not only does broccoli contain abundant amounts of vitamins A and C, but the American Institute for Cancer Research has recommended it as a food associated with lower rates of cancer—good reasons to increase your consumption of this vegetable.

1 pound broccoli
1 garlic clove, finely chopped
1 tablespoon vegetable oil
1 13-ounce can cream of
   mushroom soup
¼–½ cup milk
1 chicken bouillon cube
¾ cup shredded cheddar cheese
3 tablespoons sliced almonds

1. Cook the broccoli in 1 cup lightly salted water for about 5 minutes, or until tender. Drain. Cut into bite-size pieces.

2. Sauté the garlic in the oil for 30–60 seconds; do not brown. Add the soup and cook over medium heat, stirring continually until creamy and smooth. Add the milk and the bouillon cube. Stir until the bouillon cube is dissolved.

3. Butter the bottom and sides of a glass baking dish. Layer the broccoli and cheese, broccoli first. Pour the mushroom soup mixture over the broccoli. Sprinkle the almonds on top. Bake uncovered at 350°F. for 30 minutes, until the cheese sauce begins to bubble slowly. Serve immediately.

sautéed spring broccoli

SERVES 4–6
PREPARATION TIME:
50–60 MINUTES

Spring broccoli is different from the more common Calabrese broccoli in that it does not form heads. It also has a sharper flavor. In the Mid-Atlantic states, this broccoli is planted in the early spring and matures quickly, 45–50 days later.

1 pound spring broccoli
¼ cup chopped onion
2–3 slices uncooked bacon,
    chopped
3 tablespoons vegetable oil
1 garlic clove, finely chopped
¼ cup water
salt and pepper to taste

1. Rinse the broccoli several times in cold water to eliminate any sand. Trim off and discard any tough, thick stems.

2. Parboil the broccoli in lightly salted water for about 5 minutes. Drain. Cut into 1-inch pieces.

3. Sauté the onion and bacon in the oil for 5–10 minutes, and add the garlic and sauté for an additional 30–60 seconds. Add the water and the broccoli. Cover and cook over medium-high heat for 20–30 minutes, stirring often, until the broccoli is tender. Add more water as needed to keep the broccoli from sticking to the pan. Do not overcook. Add salt and pepper to taste, and serve hot.

kale *au gratin*

1 large bunch kale (about 1
   pound)
1 large garlic clove, chopped
2 tablespoons olive oil
2 tablespoons grated Parmesan
   cheese
2 tablespoons breadcrumbs
salt and pepper to taste

A member of the cabbage family, kale is a good source of vitamins A, B, and C. Select crisp green leaves with no signs of yellowing.

1. Rinse the kale several times in cold water to eliminate any sand. Discard the stems.

2. Bring 1–2 cups lightly salted water to a boil. Add the kale, cover, and steam over medium-high to high heat for 5–7 minutes. Drain and cut into 2-inch pieces.

3. Sauté the garlic in the oil for 30 seconds. Add the kale and 1 cup water. Cover and cook over high heat for 10 minutes or until the kale is tender. Stir often. Add the grated cheese and the breadcrumbs. Season lightly with salt and pepper. Serve immediately.

spinach frittata

SERVES 2–4
PREPARATION TIME:
30 MINUTES

Spinach is rich in vitamins A and C and contains a good deal of fiber. It matures in the cool, early spring weather, and fresh, raw spinach makes an excellent salad. However, I use frozen spinach in this recipe because of the time it saves.

A frittata is an Italian omelet—well-beaten eggs combined with any number of ingredients and cooked just until the eggs are set. The spinach and bacon or ham in this recipe are given an extra boost by the garlic.

1 cup chopped onions
2 garlic cloves, chopped
2 tablespoons vegetable oil
3 tablespoons butter
3 medium-size white potatoes,
  peeled and grated
2–3 slices uncooked bacon,
  chopped, or ¼ cup chopped
  baked Virginia ham
salt and pepper to taste
½ cup cooked chopped spinach
3 eggs
2–3 tablespoons breadcrumbs
1 tablespoon grated Parmesan
  cheese

1. Sauté the onion and garlic in the oil and butter in an 8–10-inch skillet. Add the bacon. When the bacon is cooked, add the grated potatoes. Season with salt and pepper, and cook for 8–10 minutes over medium heat. (If you're using ham instead of bacon, add it with the spinach, in step 2.)

2. Add the spinach and the ham. Add 2–3 tablespoons of water.

3. Beat the eggs and pour them over the spinach and potatoes. Top with the breadcrumbs and grated cheese. Cover and cook over low heat until the eggs are set. Cut into pie-shaped wedges and serve.

southern-style collard greens

SERVES 6
PREPARATION TIME:
60–75 MINUTES

2 pounds fresh collard greens
1 cup ham, cooked and shredded
2 garlic cloves, chopped
2 tablespoons olive oil
2–3 tablespoons vegetable oil
salt and pepper to taste
2 boiled potatoes, coarsely
  mashed

Collard greens are a good source of vitamins A and C, calcium, and potassium. They have a pleasant, mellow flavor, but they are often overlooked outside of the South. Give these a try.

1. Rinse the greens several times in cold water. Drain. Discard tough, thick stems.

2. Bring 3 cups lightly salted water to a boil. Add the greens, cover, and cook over medium-high to high heat for 15–20 minutes, or until tender. Drain. Chop into pieces.

3. Sauté the ham and the garlic in the oils for 30–60 seconds. Add the greens, cover, and cook for 30 minutes, or until tender. Add water while cooking, 1 cup at a time for a total of 1–2 cups, to keep the greens from drying out and sticking to the pan. Stir often. Season with salt and pepper to taste.

4. Add the potatoes to the greens and cook for 10–15 minutes. Serve.

cabbage with bacon

SERVES 6–8
PREPARATION TIME:
45–60 MINUTES

1 medium-size head cabbage
3–4 slices uncooked bacon,
chopped
½ medium-size onion, finely
chopped
1–2 garlic cloves, chopped
2 tablespoons oil
½ cup water
salt and pepper to taste

Fresh cabbage is available in supermarkets year round. Choose firm heads that are green, not white (the older the cabbage, the whiter the leaves appear).

1. Slice the cabbage and soak it in cold water for 5 minutes. Drain.

2. Sauté the bacon, onion, and garlic in the oil for 5–10 minutes. Add the cabbage and the water and steam over high heat in a covered pot for 20–30 minutes, or until the cabbage is tender. Stir occasionally. Add additional water as needed. Season with salt and pepper to taste, and serve.

sautéed asparagus

SERVES 4–5
PREPARATION TIME:
45 MINUTES

Select firm, green asparagus spears with tightly closed buds and as little white color at the base as possible. Asparagus is a good source of vitamins A and C. If you peel the base of the asparagus with a sharp paring knife, you won't have to discard as much of it because of toughness.

2 pounds fresh asparagus
½ medium-size onion, finely chopped
1 garlic clove, chopped
2 tablespoons vegetable oil
2 tablespoons butter
salt and pepper to taste

1. Wash the asparagus thoroughly in cold water to eliminate any sand. Snap off the tough bottom portion of the asparagus stalks and discard.

2. Parboil the asparagus in a small amount of lightly salted boiling water for 5 minutes. Drain.

3. In a skillet, sauté the onion and garlic in the oil and butter for about 3–5 minutes over medium heat. Add the asparagus. Cover and cook to the desired tenderness (5–10 minutes). Turn once, being careful not to break the stalks. Add salt and pepper to taste, and serve at once.

string bean salad

SERVES 6
PREPARATION TIME:
30–40 MINUTES

I recommend using fresh string beans, which are abundant during the summer months but can also be purchased in grocery stores periodically throughout the year. Choose tender-looking string beans that contain no enlarged beans within the pod. If fresh are not available, use frozen: never use canned.

Although this salad will keep for several days when refrigerated, it tastes best when it has just been made. The longer the salad is stored, the stronger the vinegar flavor becomes.

1½ pounds string beans
1 large garlic clove, finely
    chopped
¾ teaspoon oregano
2 tablespoons vegetable oil
1–1½ tablespoons vinegar
½ heaping tablespoon fresh
    parsley
¼ cup thinly sliced onion
1½ teaspoon salt
⅛ heaping teaspoon pepper

1. If using fresh string beans, snap off the ends and discard. Rinse thoroughly. Bring 1½ quarts of lightly salted water to a boil. Add the string beans and stir occasionally. Cook for about 15 minutes, until tender but *not* overcooked. Drain in a colander.

2. Combine all the seasonings and pour over the slightly warm string beans. Toss gently to coat the beans, being careful not to break them. Serve while still warm.

baked tomatoes

SERVES 4
PREPARATION TIME:
30–45 MINUTES

2 tablespoons vegetable oil
4 large, ripe round tomatoes,
   sliced ½-inch thick
salt and pepper to taste
sugar
¾ cup breadcrumbs
5–6 tablespoons grated Parmesan
   cheese
½–1 teaspoon oregano
½–1 teaspoon parsley flakes
3–4 garlic cloves, finely chopped
5–6 tablespoons melted butter

Select firm, unblemished, ripe round tomatoes. The best-tasting ones are undoubtedly vine ripened. Tomatoes are a delicious source of vitamins A and C.

1. Preheat the oven to 350°F.

2. Lightly grease the bottom of a baking dish with vegetable oil. Distribute the tomato slices in the dish. Season with salt, pepper, and a sprinkling of sugar.

3. Combine the breadcrumbs, cheese, oregano, parsley, garlic, and melted butter. Spoon onto the tomato slices. Cover with foil and bake for 20–30 minutes, until the tomatoes are soft. Serve.

antipasto with potatoes, peppers, and tomatoes

SERVES 4
PREPARATION TIME:
45–60 MINUTES

This is a good summertime dish, as ripe, red, juicy tomatoes are essential. Select round tomatoes or large Italian plums. Boiled potatoes and roasted sweet red peppers, flavored with garlic and other seasonings, complete this medley of tasty vegetables.

5–6 medium-size white new
   potatoes
3–4 ripe tomatoes, sliced
1 cup seasoned roasted peppers,
   sliced
5–6 tablespoons oil
3 teaspoons vinegar
1–2 teaspoons fresh parsley,
   chopped
2–3 leaves sweet basil, chopped
½ teaspoon oregano
1 garlic clove, chopped
1 teaspoon salt
⅛ teaspoon pepper

Boil the potatoes in lightly salted water for about 30 minutes, until tender (a fork should pierce the potato easily). Drain, cool slightly, remove the skins, and slice the potatoes into wedges. Add the tomato slices and roasted peppers. Mix the oil, vinegar, parsley, basil, oregano, garlic, salt, and pepper. Pour over the vegetables and toss gently. Allow the vegetables to absorb the seasonings for 15 minutes before serving. Serve at room temperature.

To Roast Peppers

Take 3–4 fresh red bell peppers (green bell peppers that have ripened on the plant and turned red). Cut the peppers in half, remove the seeds, and place cut-side down on aluminum foil. Broil until the skins turn black. Remove from the oven and place in a covered pot. Allow the peppers to steam for 10–15 minutes, then peel off and discard the blackened skins. Slice the peppers into narrow strips and season with vegetable oil, vinegar, oregano, salt, pepper, and sugar to taste. Marinate for 30–60 minutes before using.

sautéed zucchini

SERVES 4
PREPARATION TIME:
25 MINUTES

Zucchini are abundant in the summer months of July through September and are generally available in supermarkets at other times of the year. When selecting this versatile vegetable, choose only small (6–8 inches long), firm zucchini with shiny, bright green skins. Zucchini is a great food for dieters: it is rich in vitamins A and C, low in sodium, and fewer than 50 calories per cup, boiled.

2–3 medium-size zucchini
½ medium-size onion, sliced
1 garlic clove, chopped
2 tablespoons vegetable oil
2 tablespoons butter
salt and pepper to taste
grated Parmesan cheese

Wash the zucchini and slice into ¼-inch slices, unpeeled. Sauté the zucchini, onion, and garlic in the vegetable oil and butter for 7–10 minutes, until tender. Season with salt and pepper. Serve topped with grated cheese.

dad's creamed zucchini

SERVES 6
PREPARATION TIME:
50–60 MINUTES

3 medium-size zucchini, peeled
   and sliced ½-inch thick
1 garlic clove, chopped
1 teaspoon salt
¼ teaspoon pepper
1 teaspoon cinnamon
1 teaspoon allspice
2–3 tablespoons butter or
   margarine
3–4 slices stale bread, cubed
   (about 2 cups)
½ cup milk or light cream

This Northern Italian dish is pudding-like in consistency. The bread absorbs the liquid, and the cinnamon and allspice give the zucchini a unique flavor. My dad loves this dish so much he won't eat zucchini any other way.

1. Place the zucchini in a deep frying pan. Add the garlic and enough water (about 2 cups) to cover the squash. Cover and bring to a rapid boil for 5 minutes, then simmer for about 15 minutes, until the squash is tender.

2. Mash the squash until smooth, then add the salt, pepper, cinnamon, allspice, and butter. Mix well and simmer uncovered for 15–20 minutes, until the water content is reduced.

3. Add the cubed bread and simmer for 7–8 minutes.

4. Add the milk. Cook until the milk is thoroughly heated. Serve immediately.

zucchini fritters

SERVES 6–8
PREPARATION TIME:
30–40 MINUTES

1 medium-size zucchini, shred-
    ded, unpeeled (approx. 2 cups)
2 heaping tablespoons shredded
    onion
2 garlic cloves, finely chopped
2 large eggs, beaten
¾ teaspoon salt
¼ teaspoon pepper
¾ cup flour
1½ teaspoons baking powder
4 tablespoons vegetable oil

These fritters have a crisp, light, and delicate flavor.

1. Combine the zucchini, onion, garlic, eggs, salt, and pepper. Mix the flour and baking powder and add to the zucchini mixture. Stir until all the ingredients are well blended and any lumps of flour disappear. The mixture will be somewhat stiff.

2. Allow the batter to stand for 5–7 minutes while you heat the vegetable oil over high heat. Use an iron skillet, if possible, since it will allow for even cooking and maintenance of hot temperatures. The oil will be the proper temperature when it bubbles around a few drops of batter.

3. Form the fritters into tablespoon-sized portions. Flatten out the batter so that it will cook thoroughly. Cook the fritters for 3–5 minutes on each side over medium-high to high heat, until they turn a light golden brown. Drain the fritters on paper towels. Serve immediately while still warm and crisp.

extra-moist zucchini bread

SERVES 8
PREPARATION TIME:
45 MINUTES

4 teaspoons baking powder
2¼ cups prepared biscuit mixture
(with flour, shortening, baking
powder, and salt)
4 cups grated zucchini (about 2
medium-size zucchini,
unpeeled)
2 garlic cloves, finely chopped
¾ cup chopped onion
1 teaspoon oregano
1 tablespoon chopped, fresh parsley
½ teaspoon pepper
½ teaspoon salt
¼–½ cup grated Parmesan cheese
½ cup vegetable oil
5 eggs, beaten

Because of the heavy and moist texture of this bread, you must adjust the temperature and timing of the recipe to the peculiarities of your own oven, to insure that the batter cooks thoroughly.

1. Preheat the oven to 350°F.

2. Combine the baking powder and the flour mixture. Add all the remaining ingredients and stir until the lumps of flour disappear.

3. Pour the batter into a buttered glass baking dish (8″ × 12″). Bake for 30–45 minutes, until golden brown on top. It is done when a toothpick inserted into the center comes out clean. Serve warm.

min's baked cream of squash

SERVES 8
PREPARATION TIME:
60 MINUTES

This rich and flavorful dish will nicely complement a chicken or veal entrée.

1 cup thinly sliced onions
1 large garlic clove, finely
  chopped
4–5 tablespoons vegetable oil
2 tablespoons butter or margarine
6 heaping cups zucchini, peeled
  and thinly sliced
½ teaspoon salt
¼ teaspoon pepper
1 cup sour cream
1 10¾-ounce can cream of chicken
  soup
⅓–½ cup breadcrumbs
⅓ cup grated Parmesan cheese

1. Preheat the oven to 350°F.

2. Over medium heat, sauté the onions and garlic in the oil and butter for 5 minutes. Watch the onions carefully and stir often to avoid burning them.

3. Add the zucchini to the onions and garlic. Season with the salt and pepper. Cover with a lid and cook over medium-high heat for about 7 minutes, until the squash is tender. Stir often. If the squash produces too much liquid and becomes too soupy, drain off the excess liquid.

4. Place the squash in an 8" × 12" glass baking dish. Combine the sour cream and chicken soup and spoon the mixture over the squash. Sprinkle the breadcrumbs and grated cheese over the top. Cover the dish loosely with aluminum foil and bake for 30 minutes, until the liquid is set.

squash flower fritters

SERVES 4–5
PREPARATION TIME:
40–60 MINUTES

Throughout the summer months, zucchini plants produce a brilliant yellow, trumpet-shaped flower. These squash flowers are combined here with onion and garlic in a light batter to make a delightfully flavorful fritter. It is best to pick the flowers in the morning when the flowers are open and fresh with the early dew. To ensure a continuing supply of zucchini, select only the male blossoms found on thin stems. Female blossoms have a bulge at the base of the flower which will eventually develop into a squash.

30–35 squash flowers (about 1
  cup after parboiling)
2 eggs, beaten with 1–2
  tablespoons water
2 tablespoons chopped onion
1 small garlic clove, finely
  chopped
salt and pepper to taste
¼ cup flour
6–7 tablespoons vegetable oil

1. Remove all hard stems and stamen from the squash flowers. Rinse in cold water. Drain.

2. Place the squash flowers in a bowl and cover with boiling water. Allow to stand for 3–5 minutes, then drain in a colander. Squeeze out excess water from the squash flowers. Chop into small pieces.

3. Combine the eggs, onion, and garlic. Season with salt and pepper. Add the flour and mix well. Then add the squash flowers. Allow the mixture to rest for 5–10 minutes.

4. Meanwhile, heat the vegetable oil to the frying stage. The oil is ready when bubbles form around a drop of batter. Shape the batter into fritters by dropping tablespoon-size portions into the hot oil. Cook the fritters briefly until they are golden brown (3–5 minutes each side). Be sure that the batter is thoroughly cooked. Drain on paper towels. Serve immediately.

caponata

SERVES 6–8
PREPARATION TIME:
60 MINUTES

3–4 tomatoes, peeled and
   chopped
1 cup chopped celery
1 large onion, chopped (about 1
   cup)
1½ pounds eggplant, cubed, not
   peeled
vegetable oil
3 basil leaves, chopped
¼ teaspoon salt
¼ teaspoon pepper
2½ tablespoons sugar (to taste)
8 Spanish green olives, diced
1 garlic clove, finely chopped
2–3 tablespoons distilled white
   vinegar (to taste)

*If you enjoy sweet and sour foods, this Sicilian specialty should appeal to you.
It is often served cold as an antipasto.*

1. Simmer the tomatoes for 5–10 minutes. Set aside.

2. Separately fry the celery, onion, and eggplant in enough vegetable oil to cover the bottom of the pan, until tender (10–15 minutes for each). Add more oil as needed. Drain in a colander after frying.

3. Combine the eggplant, celery, onion, and tomatoes. Season with the basil, salt, pepper, and sugar to taste. Add the green olives and the garlic. Simmer over low heat (covered) for 20 minutes. Stir often. Add the vinegar and simmer for 10 more minutes. Drain off excess liquid. Serve at room temperature or chilled.

ratatouille fromage

SERVES 4–6
PREPARATION TIME:
60 MINUTES

This recipe is best when the eggplant, zucchini, tomatoes, and basil are available fresh locally—August and September in the Middle-Atlantic states. When sautéing eggplant, be aware that it can absorb vegetable oil like a sponge, resulting in an unpleasant, oily flavor. To minimize this possibility, be sure the oil is hot before you add the eggplant and use as little oil as possible.

Each vegetable in this recipe is cooked separately; any oil left over from cooking one vegetable can be used for the next, thus reducing the total amount of oil used.

1 medium-size eggplant,
   unpeeled (¾–1 pound)
½–1 cup vegetable oil
1 zucchini, unpeeled and sliced
2 tablespoons butter
1–2 garlic cloves, chopped
4 ounces sliced mushrooms
2 tablespoons fresh parsley,
   chopped
2 green peppers, thinly sliced
1 medium-size onion, chopped
   (about ¾ cup)
2–4 large Italian plum tomatoes,
   peeled and sliced (2 cups)

1. Cut the unpeeled eggplant into ½-inch cubes. Sauté in ¼–½ cup vegetable oil over medium-high to high heat until browned and somewhat soft, about 7 minutes. Stir often. Drain the eggplant with a slotted spoon and remove from the pan. Drain on paper towels.

2. Sauté the zucchini in 2–3 tablespoons vegetable oil and butter for about 5 minutes, until tender but still crisp. Remove from the pan and set aside.

3. Sauté the garlic, mushrooms, and parsley in 1–2 tablespoons vegetable oil for 2–3 minutes. Remove from the pan and set aside.

4. Fry the peppers and onion in 2–3 tablespoons vegetable oil for about 5 minutes, until they begin to turn soft. Stir often.

10–12 fresh basil leaves, chopped
  (1 tablespoon)
salt and pepper to taste
pinch sugar (optional)
6–8 slices Swiss cheese

5. Add the tomatoes to the peppers and onion. Season with basil leaves and salt and pepper. If the tomatoes are too sour, add a little sugar. Cook for about 5 minutes, until juice starts to form.

6. Lower the heat and return the eggplant, squash, and other ingredients to the pan. Simmer for 3–5 minutes to allow the flavors to blend. Turn off the heat. Place the cheese slices over the vegetables, and cover the pan with a lid. Serve when the cheese is melted.

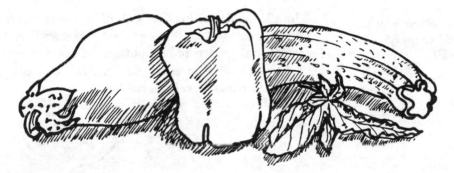

eggplant crisps

SERVES 4
PREPARATION TIME:
30–45 MINUTES

Eggplant prepared this way will be crisp and light. Serve immediately after cooking or the garlicky breadcrumb coating will lose its crispness. Whenever you cook eggplant in oil, start with just enough oil to cover the surface of the pan and add more as necessary. Cook the eggplant as quickly as possible to keep it from absorbing too much oil.

1 medium-size eggplant
½ cup flour
1 egg, beaten with 1–3 tablespoons
   water
1 cup breadcrumbs, mixed with 1
   garlic clove, finely chopped
½–1 cup vegetable oil
salt to taste

1. Peel the eggplant and slice it into lengthwise spears or into round, crosswise slices. Dust the eggplant with the flour, dip it into the egg, then coat it with the breadcrumbs and garlic.

2. In a large skillet, heat enough oil to cover the bottom of the pan. When it is hot, add the eggplant slices and fry them until tender inside and golden brown outside, about 5 minutes for each slice. Add more oil as needed. Season the cooked eggplant with salt. Drain on paper towels. Serve hot.

eggplant relish

SERVES 6
PREPARATION TIME:
30 MINUTES PLUS 1–2
HOURS TO MARINATE

3 cups water
1 cup distilled white vinegar
1 teaspoon salt
1 eggplant, peeled and shredded
  (about 3 cups)
1 teaspoon olive oil
2 tablespoons vegetable oil
1 tablespoon shredded carrot
2 tablespoons fresh parsley
1½ teaspoons oregano
2 large garlic cloves, chopped
2½ tablespoons chopped onion
2 tablespoons sugar
salt and pepper to taste

Try this as a condiment for steaks or chops. It can be stored in the refrigerator for up to two weeks.

1. Combine the water, vinegar, and salt, and bring to a boil. Remove this brine from the heat and pour it over the shredded eggplant. Allow the eggplant to absorb the brine for about 10 minutes. Then drain off all but enough brine to just cover the egglant.

2. Add all the remaining ingredients. Allow to marinate for at least 1–2 hours before serving.

pickled peppers

MAKES 5 PINTS
PREPARATION TIME:
30 MINUTES

10–12 peppers
4 cups distilled white vinegar
3 teaspoons salt
1 teaspoon pepper
2 cups sugar
5 whole, unpeeled garlic cloves

Choose red and green sweet bell peppers with firm textures and unblemished skins. You will need five pint canning jars, snap lids, and rings. The peppers can be served after 48 hours.

1. Cut the peppers into 1-inch squares.

2. Submerge the jars, lids, and rings in boiling water for about 3 minutes. Drain and set aside.

3. Bring the vinegar to a boil. Season with the salt, pepper, and sugar. Add the peppers to the hot vinegar solution for 1 minute.

4. Using a slotted spoon, remove the peppers from the vinegar solution and pack them into the hot jars. Add 1 garlic clove to each jar. Pour the vinegar solution into the jars to cover the peppers. Place the lids and rings on the jars. The jars are sealed when the lids snap.

beet salad

SERVES 6–8
PREPARATION TIME:
60 MINUTES PLUS 30
MINUTES TO MARINATE

12 fresh beets, sliced (about 1
quart)
1 teaspoon salt
½ teaspoon pepper
1 small garlic clove, finely
chopped
⅓ cup sliced onion
1 teaspoon sugar
1 sprig fresh parsley, chopped
(about 1 tablespoon)
3 tablespoons distilled white
vinegar
4 tablespoons vegetable oil
5 tablespoons water
¼ teaspoon oregano

Select beets that are firm and well rounded, dark red with bright green tops and no sign of wilting. Don't throw away the beet tops—they can be cooked and served in the same manner as spinach.

1. Cut off the green beet tops 1 inch above the beet. Wash the beets in cold water. Drain. Place the beets in a large stock pot and cover with water. Bring to a boil. Reduce the heat and cook at a low boil (covered) until tender (fork will pierce beets easily), about 60 minutes. Drain and cool. Slip off the skins and discard.

2. Slice the beets thin. Combine all the remaining ingredients and pour the mixture over the beets. Toss. Allow the beets to stand for about 30 minutes before serving so the seasonings can blend and be absorbed by the beets.

stuffed mushrooms

SERVES 8–10
PREPARATION TIME:
60 MINUTES

1½ pounds mushrooms (about 40)
4 slices uncooked bacon
4 medium garlic cloves, chopped
1 teaspoon parsley flakes
1 heaping tablespoon chopped
   onion
salt and pepper to taste
½ pound sweet Italian sausage
¾ cup breadcrumbs
2 tablespoons butter

Fresh mushrooms are available year round. Choose firm, snow-white mushrooms with fairly tight caps and light, tan-colored gills. Mushrooms may be refrigerated up to one week, but it is best to use them as soon after purchasing as possible.

1. Preheat the oven to 325°F.

2. Wipe the mushrooms with a damp paper towel. Discard a thin slice from the bottom of each stem. Break off the stems, chop up, and set aside. Reserve the caps.

3. Cook the bacon until crisp, remove from the pan, drain, and crumble into small pieces. Sauté the garlic, chopped mushroom stems, parsley, and onion in 1–2 tablespoons bacon fat. Sprinkle lightly with salt and pepper, if desired.

4. Remove the sausage from its casing and break it up into small pieces. Fry in a separate pan for 10–15 minutes, until browned. Add the mushroom mixture, bacon, breadcrumbs, and a few tablespoons of water, and simmer for 2–3 minutes.

5. Place the mushroom caps bottom up on a cookie tray lined with aluminum foil. Place a small piece of butter in each cap. Then fill each cap with the mushroom and sausage mixture and bake for 30 minutes. Serve at once.

wild mushrooms

SERVES 4
PREPARATION TIME:
45–60 MINUTES

Due to their limited availability and distinctive taste, wild mushrooms are considered a delicacy. Mushroom hunting requires the knowledge to distinguish edible varieties from poisonous ones growing in forests and fields. I rely on trustworthy friends who are experienced mushroom hunters to supply the main ingredient for this recipe. Do not attempt to pick wild mushrooms for eating unless you are absolutely certain that you know what you are doing.

1 pound wild mushrooms
2–3 large garlic cloves, finely
   chopped
½ green pepper, diced
4–5 tablespoons vegetable oil
1 tablespoon butter
salt and black pepper to taste
1 tablespoon parsley, chopped
pinch crushed red pepper
pinch oregano
2 links sweet Italian sausage,
   cooked and cut up
½–1 cup tomato sauce (from
   Mom's Tomato Sauce and
   Meatballs, page 82) or 1 cup
   peeled and sliced fresh
   tomatoes

1. Clean and trim the mushrooms. Rinse several times in cold water to eliminate any sand. Parboil for 8–10 minutes. Drain. Rinse with cold water and drain again.

2. Sauté the garlic and green pepper in oil and butter. Add the mushrooms, season with salt, black pepper, parsley, red pepper, and oregano, and cook for 7–10 minutes. Add the sausage, cover, and cook over low to medium heat for 30 minutes, stirring often. Add the tomato sauce and simmer, covered, for 30–40 minutes, stirring occasionally. If the mixture seems too dry, add a little water from time to time as the mushrooms cook. Serve hot.

baked stuffed potatoes

SERVES 8–10
PREPARATION TIME:
90 MINUTES

8–12 Idaho potatoes
3 tablespoons butter or margarine
salt and pepper to taste
1 slice Monterey Jack cheese per
  potato (at room temperature)
1 small garlic clove, finely
  chopped
1–1¼ cups milk (at room
  temperature)

Use large Idaho potatoes for this recipe. Select firm potatoes with smooth skins and no sign of sprouting. You may substitute other cheeses, such as Muenster or Swiss, for variety.

1. Preheat the oven to 375°F. and bake the potatoes for 1 hour or longer, until they are cooked (when easily pierced with a fork). When the potatoes are done, reduce the oven temperature to 350°F.

2. Cut the potatoes in half lengthwise. Scoop out the pulp, being careful not to damage the potato skins. Leave a thin layer of potato pulp attached to the potato skins.

3. Use an electric mixer to whip the potatoes. When they are smooth, add the butter, salt and pepper, cheese, and garlic. After all the ingredients are well blended, add the milk a little at a time and beat until smooth, creamy, and thick, but not too stiff. Adjust the amount of milk accordingly. Scoop the potato mixture into the potato skins.

4. Place on a cookie tray and bake at 350°F. for 15 minutes, or until the potatoes are puffy and lightly golden. Serve immediately; otherwise, the potatoes will shrink.

parmesan potato fritters

SERVES 4
PREPARATION TIME:
30 MINUTES

2 cups mashed potatoes
2 tablespoons fresh parsley,
   chopped
1 small garlic clove, finely
   chopped
4–5 tablespoons grated Parmesan
   cheese
2 eggs, beaten
salt and pepper to taste
breadcrumbs
vegetable oil

This is a great recipe for using leftover mashed potatoes—quick, easy, and flavorful.

1. Mix the mashed potatoes with the parsley, garlic, grated cheese, eggs, and salt and pepper. Form into patties and coat with the breadcrumbs. If the mixture is too soft to form patties, add more mashed potatoes.

2. In a large skillet, heat enough vegetable oil to cover the bottom of the pan. Add more as needed. Fry the fritters in the hot oil until golden brown. Turn over only once to avoid breaking. Serve immediately.

potato salad

SERVES 6–8
PREPARATION TIME:
60 MINUTES

Try this salad with new potatoes—those harvested in late winter or early spring with thin, paper-like, brown or red skins. Potatoes contain vitamin C, which is water soluble, so to retard the dissolution and evaporation of this vitamin, boil the potatoes with the skins on or steam them.

2¼ pounds potatoes
3 eggs
½–1 teaspoon salt
⅛ teaspoon pepper
3 tablespoons vegetable oil
3 tablespoons vinegar
⅓ cup chopped celery
2 tablespoons chopped onion
1 small garlic clove, finely
  chopped
1 tablespoon fresh parsley,
  chopped
¼ cup India sweet relish
1 cup mayonnaise
3 tablespoons milk

1. Boil the potatoes in lightly salted water for 20 minutes, or until you can easily pierce the potato with a fork. Peel, then cut the potatoes into cubes. Meanwhile, hard-boil the eggs. Cool and grate them.

2. Season the potatoes with salt, pepper, oil, and vinegar. Add the celery, onion, garlic, parsley, and relish. Mix the mayonnaise with the milk until smooth. Pour over the potatoes and eggs. Toss until all the ingredients are well blended. Serve at room temperature or chilled.

macaroni salad

SERVES 6–8
PREPARATION TIME:
30 MINUTES

7 ounces elbow macaroni (2
 cups)
½ cup mayonnaise
1 tablespoon oil
2–2½ teaspoons vinegar
1 garlic clove, chopped
3 hard-boiled eggs, chopped
1 carrot, grated
1 heaping teaspoon chopped
 onion
½ cup chopped celery
1 tablespoon fresh parsley,
 chopped
4 tablespoons India relish
salt and pepper to taste

For easy-to-peel hard-boiled eggs, try the following: Cover eggs in a pan with water at least an inch above the eggs. Bring the water to a rolling boil, remove the pan from the heat, cover, and let stand for 15–20 minutes. Drain, then cool the eggs thoroughly in cold water. Roll the egg on a hard surface to loosen the shell, then peel from the large end of the egg. The shells should come off easily.

1. Add the macaroni to 2 quarts boiling, lightly salted water. Boil for 6–8 minutes. Do not overcook; macaroni should be *al dente*. Drain. Rinse in cold water. Drain again.

2. Combine the mayonnaise with the oil and vinegar. Pour over the macaroni. Add all the remaining ingredients. Mix well and serve.

ceci bean salad

SERVES 4–6
PREPARATION TIME:
30 MINUTES PLUS OVER-
NIGHT TO MARINATE
AND 1 HOUR TO SET

½–¾ cup water (or enough to
   cover ceci beans)
¼ cup plus 1 tablespoon white
   wine vinegar
¼ cup sugar
⅛ teaspoon salt
pepper to taste
20 ounces canned ceci beans,
   drained
2 tablespoons chopped celery
   (tender stalks and leaves)
1 small garlic clove, finely
   chopped
1 heaping tablespoon chopped
   onion
several pieces sweet red pepper

Ceci beans, also known as chick peas or garbanzo beans, are round and buff colored—somewhat similar in size, shape, and color to macadamia nuts. You should begin this recipe a day ahead of time, since the beans must be marinated overnight.

1. Bring the water, vinegar, sugar, salt, and pepper to a boil. Cover and reduce to a low boil for about 5 minutes. Cover the ceci beans with this liquid. Allow to cool to room temperature, then marinate the beans overnight in the refrigerator.

2. The next day, add the remaining ingredients. Allow the beans to absorb the flavor of all ingredients for an hour before serving. Serve at room temperature or chilled.

vegetarian melt

SERVES 4
PREPARATION TIME:
30 MINUTES

2 zucchini, sliced
1 garlic clove, finely chopped
1 small onion, sliced
2 carrots, peeled, julienned
1 large bell pepper, thinly sliced
2 tablespoons vegetable oil
3–4 tablespoons butter
salt and pepper to taste
4 slices pumpernickel bread
4 slices Swiss cheese

This is a very adaptable recipe. Experiment with any combination of vegetables, or substitute wheat or rye breads or other cheeses, such as mozzarella or Monterey jack.

1. Preheat the oven to 375°F.

2. Sauté the vegetables in the oil and butter for 5–7 minutes, until tender but still crisp. Season lightly with salt and pepper. Remove from the pan with a slotted spoon. Drain on paper towels.

3. Distribute the vegetables over the slices of bread. Top with Swiss cheese. Place in the warm oven until the cheese melts. Serve immediately.

Soups

The air of Provence was "particularly perfumed by the refined essence of this mystically attractive bulb."

Alexandre Dumas

Soups may be delectably seasoned by garlic, as suggested in these recipes. Whole cloves simmered in soup stock will impart a mild garlic flavor to the broth. Finely chopped garlic sautéed with vegetables will delicately season any soup stock. Garlic may also be used as a flavoring for meat fillings in pastas which may be added to soups.

Many of the following soup recipes are traditionally associated with certain seasons of the year or certain holidays. Fresh Vegetable Soup and Peas and Pasta Soup are light soups usually reserved for summer meals. I enjoy the heartier soups such as Tripe Soup and Lentil Soup for fall or winter meals. Meatless soups such as Mushroom Velvet and Cream of Broccoli Soup are well suited for lenten repasts or for vegetarian diets, whereas Escarole Soup and Tortellini Soup are enjoyed as Christmas favorites by some Italian families. There is really no reason, however, save for seasonal unavailability of some ingredients, that you need restrict yourself to any particular timetable.

The following soups can be prepared fairly quickly and thus are good for days when you do not have a lot of time to spend in the kitchen: Pasta e Fagioli, Corn and Clam Chowder, and Cream of Asparagus Soup. For those soups that take longer, keep in mind that for most of that time the soup is merely simmering, and not requiring attention from the cook.

Some of the soup recipes presented here are large-batch sizes. You can make the soup stock ahead of time, and freeze it in smaller portions until you are ready to use it. When pasta is called for, add it when you reheat the soup stock for serving. Otherwise, the pasta may be overcooked and may also absorb too much of the soup broth.

glorious garlic soup

SERVES 4
PREPARATION TIME:
60 MINUTES

1 medium onion, sliced
10 cloves of garlic, finely chopped
4 tablespoons butter
1 teaspoon vegetable oil
1–2 tablespoons fresh parsley
   (chopped)
salt and pepper, to taste
4 cups water
4 chicken bouillon cubes
4 slices Italian or French bread
   (optional)
4 slices Swiss cheese

1. Sauté onion and garlic in butter and oil until the onion is soft. Do not brown. Add parsley, salt, and pepper.

2. Pour in 4 cups water and bring to a boil. Add bouillon cubes and simmer, covered with a lid, for 30 minutes.

Optional: Broil bread on both sides until crisp. Turn off broiler, and then place slices of cheese on the bread. Keep the bread in the oven until the cheese melts. Place one slice of bread on top of each individual serving of soup. Serve immediately.

asparagus and rice soup

SERVES 4–6
PREPARATION TIME:
30–40 MINUTES

3 cups chopped asparagus
1 garlic clove, chopped
1 small onion, chopped (about ¼
  cup)
½ cup uncooked rice
1 chicken bouillon cube
2 tablespoons olive oil
1½ teaspoons salt
⅛ teaspoon pepper
2 tablespoons butter

Asparagus is rich in vitamins A and C. Look for tender, bright green stalks. To prepare asparagus discard the tough base of the spears, and rinse the remaining stalks well to remove all trace of sand.

Bring 4½ cups water to a boil. Add the asparagus, garlic, onion, rice, bouillon cube, oil, salt, and pepper. Return to a boil. Then reduce the heat to low. Cover and cook until the rice is tender, about 20 minutes. Stir often. Do not overcook. Add the butter. Serve hot.

tripe soup

SERVE 8–10
PREPARATION TIME:
2½–3 HOURS

For decades, tripe has been popular among certain ethnic peoples such as southern blacks, Italians, and Mexican Americans. Recently, the wisdom of these tastes has been recognized by others and the use of tripe elevated to the level of gourmet dining. The unique flavor of tripe is highlighted by garlic in this peppery, thick, and very substantial soup. For this recipe, purchase frozen honeycomb tripe, which has been blanched and parboiled. Have your butcher cut the tripe into ½-inch strips, and keep it frozen until you are ready to use it.

Step #1 of this recipe can be completed a day ahead of time and the tripe refrigerated overnight.

4 pounds frozen tripe
5 pounds white potatoes, peeled
   and cubed
2 cups sliced onion
1 garlic clove, chopped
1–2 tablespoons vegetable oil
5 tablespoons butter
1 teaspoon salt
½ teaspoon pepper
1½–2 teaspoons nutmeg
butter to taste

1. Cut the frozen tripe into ½-inch cubes. Rinse in cold water. Drain. The tripe must be boiled three times and the water discarded after each boiling. For the first two times, add the tripe to rapidly boiling water and boil for 10 minutes each time. For the final boiling, add the tripe to rapidly boiling water, lower to simmer, and cook for 25 minutes or longer, until tender. Drain. The texture of the tripe will be soft and spongy, and its volume reduced considerably.

2. Meanwhile, boil the potatoes in 3 quarts lightly salted water until tender. Keep the pot covered so the water does not evaporate while cooking; this water will serve as the soup base. When the potatoes are cooked, mash them in the water in which they were cooked.

3. Sauté the onion and garlic in the oil and butter until the onion is soft. Add the tripe and season with salt, pepper, and nutmeg.

Cook for 40–60 minutes over medium heat. Add the tripe mixture to the potato soup base and cook over low heat (covered) for 30 minutes or longer, until the tripe is soft and tender. Just before serving, add butter to taste.

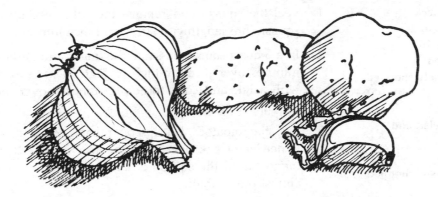

italian long-neck squash soup

SERVES 8
PREPARATION TIME:
50–60 MINUTES

Italian "long-neck" squash are light green. They grow in a slightly curved shape, 2 to 3 feet in length and about 3 inches in diameter. These squash may be purchased in late summer from farmers' produce stands. Their flavor is delicate and distinctively different from zucchini.

5 cups Italian long-neck
   squash, diced (about 2
   medium-size squash)
¼ cup chopped onion
1–2 garlic cloves, finely chopped
2 tablespoons vegetable oil
1 tablespoon olive oil
2 cups tomatoes, peeled and
   sliced
⅛ teaspoon pepper
2 teaspoons fresh basil, chopped
½ scant teaspoon salt
½ teaspoon sugar (to taste)
¾–1 cup spaghetti, broken into
   1-inch pieces
½ teaspoon salt (optional)
grated Parmesan cheese

1. Peel the squash and remove the soft, seed-filled center. Cut the squash into lengthwise strips and dice into ½-inch pieces.

2. In a 3-quart saucepan, sauté the onion and garlic in the oils for 2–3 minutes over medium-high to high heat. Add the squash, cover with a lid, and cook for 10–12 minutes over medium-high heat, stirring frequently.

3. Add the tomatoes, black pepper, basil, ½ teaspoon salt, and sugar, if needed. Cook over medium heat (covered) for 30 minutes or longer, until the squash is tender. Stir often. The squash will be almost transparent.

4. Add 1–1½ cups water to the squash mixture and bring it to a rapid boil. Add the spaghetti and ½ teaspoon salt (if desired) and cook together for about 7 minutes, until the spaghetti is *al dente* tender. If the soup appears too thick, add more water. Serve topped with grated cheese.

fresh vegetable soup

SERVES 8
PREPARATION TIME:
60 MINUTES

This light summer soup is a flavorful way of using the vegetables that abound in mid- to late summer. You can use whatever vegetables are available in your part of the country at any time of year.

5 slices uncooked bacon, chopped
1 cup chopped onion
2 large garlic cloves, finely chopped
2 tablespoons butter
1–2 tablespoons vegetable oil
2 carrots, peeled and diced
2 celery stalks and leaves, diced
4 cups white potatoes, cubed and
    parboiled for 15–20 minutes
3 cups tomatoes, peeled, chopped
2 beef bouillon cubes
1 chicken bouillon cube
2 cups corn
2 cups zucchini, cut in ½-inch cubes
2 bay leaves
¼ teaspoon thyme
1 tablespoon basil, chopped
2 tablespoons fresh parsley,
    chopped
salt and pepper to taste

In a large stockpot, sauté the bacon, onion, and garlic in butter and oil until the onion becomes soft (8–10 minutes). Add the carrots, celery, and potatoes and sauté for 5–8 minutes. Add the tomatoes. Dissolve the three bouillon cubes in 3 cups water and pour into the soup. Then add the corn, zucchini, bay leaves, thyme, basil, and parsley. Season with salt and pepper. Simmer for 30 minutes, or until the potatoes are cooked. Add more water if necessary. Serve.

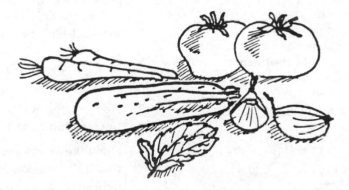

lentil soup

SERVES 8
PREPARATION TIME:
1½–2 HOURS

1 pound lentils
½ cup fat (from baked ham)
2 tablespoons oil
½ cup chopped onion
2 garlic cloves, chopped
½ cup chopped celery
3 carrots, thinly sliced
2 tablespoons fresh parsley,
   chopped
1 bay leaf
salt and pepper to taste
1 ham bone
1 cup cubed baked ham
1 cup fresh tomatoes, peeled and
   chopped
1 beef bouillon cube

Lentils are rich in protein and are excellent in soups such as this one, which is good for using up the leftovers from a dinner of baked Virginia ham.

1. Rinse the lentils in cold water. Place them in a 3-quart saucepan and cover with about 1 quart cold water. Boil the lentils in a covered pot for 3 minutes. If you are using an electric burner, turn off the heat and let the pot stand on the burner for 15 minutes, until water is absorbed and the lentils have plumped up. With a gas range, continue to cook over low heat for about 7 minutes, and then allow the lentils to stand for 15 minutes or until plump.

2. Meanwhile, sauté the ham fat in oil in a large stockpot. Add the onion, garlic, celery, carrots, parsley, and bay leaf. Sauté over medium-high heat until the vegetables are tender, 10–20 minutes. Season with salt and pepper. Add the ham bone and the pieces of ham. Cook for 5–10 minutes. Add the tomatoes and cook for 10 more minutes.

3. Add enough water to cover the vegetables (1 quart or more). Add the bouillon cube and cook for 10–15 minutes.

4. Drain the lentils and add them to the vegetable stock, making sure that there is enough liquid to cover them. Add additional water if necessary. Bring to a rapid boil, then reduce the heat and simmer for about 60 minutes, covered.

pasta and beef soup

SERVES 6–8
PREPARATION TIME:
30 MINUTES PLUS 2½
HOURS TO SIMMER

1 pound beef chuck neck bones
1 pound boneless beef hind
　shanks
2 beef bouillon cubes
1 medium-size onion, cut into
　large pieces
1 garlic clove, chopped
2 whole carrots, peeled
1 stalk celery, in big chunks, with
　leaves
5–6 cherry tomtoes
1 teaspoon parsley, chopped
4–6 ounces thin noodles, broken
　into 1-inch pieces
salt to taste
grated Parmesan cheese

Select the meatiest neck bones or other beef soup bones you can find. The neck bones and hind shank cuts specified in this recipe are relatively inexpensive cuts of meat. The slow simmering of the broth makes them quite tender.

1. Rinse the neck bones and beef shanks in water. Drain. Trim and discard gristle.

2. Add the meat to 3 quarts lightly salted boiling water. Skim off any foam that forms on top of the soup.

3. Allow the soup to boil slowly (covered) for about 2 hours, or until the meat is tender and will easily fall off the bone. Remove the meat from the soup, shred it into pieces, and set aside. Discard the bones.

4. Add the bouillon cubes, onion, garlic, carrots, celery, tomatoes, and parsley to the soup stock. Cook an additional 30–40 minutes. You may need to add more water if too much of the broth evaporates. Return the shredded meat to the soup stock.

5. In a separate pot, add the noodles to rapidly boiling lightly salted water. Boil for 5 minutes, or until the noodles are cooked to the *al dente* stage. Drain. Place the noodles in soup plates, and spoon the broth over them. Top with grated cheese and serve.

hearty bean soup

SERVES 8
PREPARATION TIME:
60–90 MINUTES PLUS 2½–3
HOURS TO SIMMER

16 ounces dried, small white
   beans
3–4 slices uncooked bacon, diced
   (about ¼ cup)
2–3 tablespoons vegetable oil
2 garlic cloves, chopped
1½ cups chopped celery
½ cup chopped carrots
½ cup chopped onion
1 tablespoon fresh parsley,
   chopped
2 large smoked pork hocks (about
   1½ pounds)
3 beef bouillon cubes
1 teaspoon salt
½ teaspoon thyme
1 medium-size tomato, with skin,
   cubed
10 ounces frozen chopped spinach
¼–⅓ cup small pasta (e.g., tubetini)
salt and pepper to taste

This recipe creates a nutritious and flavorful soup from inexpensive ingredients: dried white beans, a good source of protein, and pork hocks (cross sections of the animal's leg), an often ignored cut of pork. If pork hocks are not available, you can substitute a meaty, cooked ham bone.

1. Rinse the beans in cold water. Discard any foreign substances, such as particles of soil. Place the beans in a pot with enough water to cover. Bring the water to a boil and boil (covered) for 5–10 minutes. Turn off the burner, keep the lid on the pot, and allow the beans to absorb the water for 10–15 minutes.

2. Meanwhile, sauté the bacon in about 1 tablespoon vegetable oil for 3–4 minutes. Add the garlic and sauté about 1 minute longer. Add the celery, carrots, onion, parsley, and remaining vegetable oil. Season lightly with salt and pepper. Continue sautéing until the vegetables are tender, about 15–20 minutes.

3. Rinse the pork hocks in warm water. Drain. Using a sharp knife, score the skin of the hocks lengthwise at 2-inch intervals. Place the hocks in a large stockpot and cover with water (2–2½ quarts). Add the sautéed vegetables and bring the soup stock to a boil.

4. Pour the beans and the water in which they were cooked into the soup stock. Add the bouillon cubes, salt, thyme, and tomato. Cover and cook over low heat for 2½–3 hours, until the beans are soft, stirring periodically.

5. Cook the spinach and the pasta, each according to package directions. Drain. Add them to the soup for the last 10 minutes of cooking time.

6. While the spinach and pasta are cooking, remove the 2 pork hocks from the soup with tongs or a slotted spoon. Cut the pork off the bone and into bite-size pieces. Then return the pieces of pork to the soup, heat through, and serve.

escarole soup

SERVES 6–8
PREPARATION TIME:
30–40 MINUTES PLUS OVER-
NIGHT TO CHILL STOCK
AND 1¾ HOURS TO SIMMER

Chicken stock:

2–3 chicken backs (about 1½ pounds)
2 teaspoons salt
1 chicken bouillon cube
1 small onion, halved
1 stalk celery, cut into 3-inch pieces
2 cherry tomatoes
1 carrot, peeled
2 sprigs parsley, chopped (2–3 tablespoons)
1 whole garlic clove
2 heads escarole (about 3 pounds)

Escarole is a member of the endive family. It has broad, wavy leaves and is rich in vitamin A, calcium, and iron. Select firm heads, bright green in color.

The escarole may be blanched and frozen until ready to use, and the meatballs may be frozen, uncooked, until they are needed. Prepare the stock for this soup a day ahead, but omit the escarole and meatballs until the next day. The relatively sharp taste of escarole is transformed by this soup stock.

1. Rinse the chicken backs in cold water. Trim off excess fat. Drain.

2. Bring 2 quarts water to a boil. Add the chicken and the salt. Skim off any foam that forms. Then add all the remaining ingredients except the escarole and the meatballs. Simmer (covered) for 1 hour.

3. Remove the chicken backs from the soup, remove the meat from the bones, discard skin and bones, and return the chicken to the soup. Allow the stock to cool, then refrigerate overnight.

4. On the following day, discard the layer of fat that forms on the surface of the cold chicken stock, using a spatula or a wooden spoon. Reheat the stock. While the stock is simmering, prepare the escarole. Discard the tough, outer, dark green leaves. Trim the tough tips of the remaining leaves. Cut the escarole into 1–2-inch pieces. Rinse thoroughly in cold water several times to remove any sand. Bring 5 quarts lightly salted water to a boil. Add the escarole and boil for 5–7 minutes. Drain. Rinse in cold water. Squeeze out excess water and set aside.

Meatballs:

1 slice day-old Italian bread
⅛ cup milk
½ pound lean ground beef
1 large egg, beaten
½ teaspoon salt
⅛ teaspoon black pepper
1 garlic clove, chopped
1½ tablespoons grated
  Parmesan cheese
2 teaspoons fresh parsley, chopped
breadcrumbs (optional)

5. Prepare the meatballs. Soak the bread in the milk, squeeze out excess milk, and crumble into small pieces. Mix the bread with all the remaining ingredients, adding some breadcrumbs if the mixture is too soft. Shape into approximately 40 1-inch balls and add to the simmering soup. Cook for 5–7 minutes.

6. Add the escarole and simmer, covered, at a low boil for 45 minutes, or until the escarole is tender. Serve topped with grated Parmesan cheese.

cabbage soup

SERVES 4–6
PREPARATION TIME:
60–90 MINUTES

½ medium-size head cabbage,
shredded (6 cups)
3 slices uncooked bacon, diced
⅓ cup chopped onion
1 garlic clove, finely chopped
1 tablespoon vegetable oil
1 quart chicken stock
1 tablespoon chicken fat
(optional)
1 medium-size tomato, peeled
and sliced (1 cup)
salt and pepper to taste
1 large white potato, peeled and
cut into small cubes
½ teaspoon thyme

Select firm and heavy cabbage heads. Avoid heads that are mostly white in color or dried around the core, signs of old age. Cabbage is rich in vitamin C.

1. Rinse the cabbage in cold water.

2. In a large stockpot, sauté the bacon, onion, and garlic in the oil for 5–7 minutes, until the onion is soft.

3. Add the chicken stock, chicken fat, and tomato. When the broth begins to boil, add the cabbage and season with salt and pepper (start with 1 teaspoon salt, ¼ teaspoon pepper). Cook, covered, over high heat for about 5 minutes. Lower to a medium boil for 15–20 minutes, stirring often.

4. Add the potatoes, season with thyme, and continue to cook at a medium boil for an additional 30–35 minutes, or until the cabbage and potatoes are tender. Add more water, about 1 cup or so, as needed. Serve hot.

mushroom velvet

SERVES 4
PREPARATION TIME:
30–40 MINUTES

With soup this good, your dinner guests will think you spent hours in the kitchen. The truth is that, if you have chicken stock on hand, this soup can be made in less than an hour.

1 garlic clove, finely chopped
⅓–½ cup chopped onion
2 tablespoons butter
½ teaspoon vegetable oil
8 ounces mushrooms, chopped
salt and pepper to taste
5 tablespoons butter
5 tablespoons flour
1 cup milk
14 ounces chicken stock
½ teaspoon fresh parsley,
  chopped
½ cup heavy cream
chives

1. Sauté the garlic and onion in 2 tablespoons butter and oil for 3–5 minutes, until the onion becomes transparent. Add the finely chopped mushrooms, season with salt and pepper, and sauté for 3–5 minutes longer.

2. Melt 5 tablespoons butter in a saucepan. As the butter begins to bubble, add the flour and blend it in quickly. Allow the butter and flour to thicken, while stirring constantly for about 1 minute. Add the milk, a little at a time, mixing well to avoid lumps. Allow the liquid to cook over medium heat until it thickens and bubbles (5–7 minutes).

3. Add the chicken stock, the mushroom mixture, and the parsley. Simmer for about 5 minutes. Remove from the heat, add the heavy cream. Serve topped with chives.

corn and clam chowder

SERVES 4
PREPARATION TIME:
45 MINUTES

Corn tastes best when eaten as soon after harvesting as possible, since the sugar in corn begins turning to starch once it is picked. If you can view the kernels before selecting your corn, look for bright yellow, evenly spaced kernels. To select corn without viewing the kernels (some grocers discourage peeking), look for bright green husks with no sign of dryness.

3 slices uncooked bacon, diced
1 tablespoon butter
2 garlic cloves, finely chopped
1 heaping tablespoon chopped
   onion
1 heaping tablespoon fresh
   parsley, chopped
2 cups water
1 chicken bouillon cube
2 cups fresh corn (about 3 ears)
3 tablespoons flour
1 cup milk
1 6¼-ounce can minced clams
3 tablespoons heavy cream
salt and pepper to taste
1 tablespoon butter

1. Sauté the bacon in a large stockpot with 1 tablespoon butter, until browned. Add the garlic, onion, and parsley, and sauté until the onion is tender.

2. Add the water and bouillon cube and simmer for 5 minutes.

3. Add the corn and cook over medium heat for 10–15 minutes, until the corn is tender.

4. Mix the flour with ¼ cup of the milk until smooth. Add to the soup. Add the remaining milk.

5. Drain the minced clams and add the clam juice to the soup. Simmer for 3–4 minutes.

6. Add the heavy cream and simmer for 1–2 minutes. Remove from the heat, add the clams and allow them to heat through. Season with salt and pepper and 1 tablespoon butter. Serve immediately.

clam bisque

SERVES 6–8
PREPARATION TIME:
60 MINUTES

This soup is rich and delicious. Although you can use fresh clams, I suggest that it is easier and just as flavorful to use canned, minced clams. Do not overcook the clams, or they will become tough. Add them to the soup just before serving.

2 garlic cloves, chopped
½ cup chopped onion
½ cup chopped celery
2 slices uncooked bacon, chopped
3 tablespoons butter
2 chicken bouillon cubes
4–5 medium-size potatoes, peeled
   and cut into ½-inch cubes
   (about 2½ cups)
1–2 cups frozen mixed vegetables, or
   ½ cup each fresh peas, corn, and
   chopped carrots, blanched
1 bay leaf
½ teaspoon thyme
½ teaspoon parsley, chopped
1 teaspoon salt
⅛ teaspoon pepper
⅓–½ cup flour
1¼ cups milk
½–¾ cup heavy cream
16 ounces minced clams

1. Sauté the garlic, onion, celery, and bacon in butter for 5–7 minutes. Stir often.

2. Bring 1 quart water to boil in a large stockpot. Add the sautéed mixture, bouillon cubes, potatoes, and mixed vegetables. Season with the bay leaf, thyme, parsley, salt, and pepper. Allow to cook at a slow boil until all the vegetables are tender (20–25 minutes). Add up to 1 cup water if necessary.

3. Combine the flour with ¼ cup of the milk. Blend until the consistency is very smooth. Add to the soup. Allow to simmer for 3–4 minutes. Add the remaining milk and the cream. Simmer uncovered for only about 2 minutes.

4. Add the minced clams and the juice in which they are packed. If the soup is too thick, dilute with additional milk. Remove from the heat. Serve when the clams are warmed through.

cream of broccoli soup

SERVES 4
PREPARATION TIME:
60 MINUTES

½ cup chopped onion
2 garlic cloves, finely chopped
1 small carrot, shredded
3 tablespoons butter
1 teaspoon vegetable oil
salt and pepper to taste
4 tablespoons butter
4 tablespoons flour
1 cup milk
2 cups water
2 chicken bouillon cubes
8–10 ounces fresh broccoli spears,
  chopped
½ cup heavy cream

For this soup, select broccoli with tightly closed buds and a bright green color. Discard the thick woody stems, which tend to be tough and fibrous.

1. Sauté the onion, garlic, and carrot in 3 tablespoons butter and 1 teaspoon oil for 5–6 minutes over medium to medium-high heat, until the onion becomes transparent. Season lightly with salt and pepper. Remove from the heat and set aside.

2. Prepare a roux by melting 4 tablespoons butter over low heat. Add the flour and stir briskly, allowing the mixture to bubble rapidly and thicken. Add the milk, a little at a time, stirring constantly to keep lumps from forming as the mixture thickens. Remove from the heat.

3. In a separate saucepan, bring 2 cups water and the bouillon cubes to a boil. Add this broth to the roux, a little at a time, stirring continuously.

4. Cook the broccoli in rapidly boiling unsalted water (2 cups) for about 7 minutes, until tender. Drain. Add the broccoli and other cooked vegetables to the soup base. If the soup is too thick, add a little more water. Cook on low for 7–10 minutes, covered. Just before serving, remove from the heat and add the cream. Serve at once.

tortellini broth

MAKES 2 BATCHES OF
6–8 SERVINGS
PREPARATION TIME:
1¾–2 HOURS
NOT INCLUDING
TORTELLINI

2 chicken breasts, or 3 chicken
  backs (1–1½ pounds)
1 pound beef spare ribs
2 chicken bouillon cubes
½ medium-size onion, sliced
1 garlic clove, peeled
1 tablespoon fresh parsley,
  chopped
2 stalks celery, cut into 3–4-inch
  pieces
1–2 carrots, peeled and cut into
  3–4-inch pieces
¼–½ teaspoon pepper
½ cup escarole, chopped, blanched
  (optional)
16 ounces tortellini
grated Parmesan cheese

The base for this soup is a good, old-fashioned chicken broth with some beef added for additional flavor. The tortellini you use may be commercially prepared with any number of different fillings, or, if you prefer, you can make your own according to the recipe on page 92. This recipe makes enough broth for two batches, each enough for 6–8 servings. The tortellini called for is only enough for one batch. If you want to serve two batches' worth, double the amount of tortellini in the list of ingredients.

1. Rinse the chicken and spare ribs in cold water. Drain on paper towels. Trim off excess chicken fat.

2. Place the chicken and spare ribs in 5–6 quarts lightly salted water. Bring to a rapid boil. When foam appears on top of the broth, skim it off. Reduce the heat to simmer, add the bouillon cubes, onion, garlic, parsley, celery, carrots, and pepper. Cook for 60–90 minutes (covered). Remove the meat from the soup. Cut the meat from the bones, discard the bones, and return the meat to the soup.

3. Add the escarole. Cook 20 minutes longer. Add additional water if the broth evaporates. Discard the celery.

4. Set aside half of the broth to freeze. To the other half add 16 ounces tortellini and simmer, covered, for 25–30 minutes (fresh homemade pasta will take less time) or until the pasta is tender. Serve topped with Parmesan cheese.

pasta e fagioli

SERVES 4–6
PREPARATION TIME:
2–2½ HOURS, PLUS OVER-
NIGHT SOAKING OF
BEANS

1 cup dry northern white beans
4 cups water
½ teaspoon salt
1 tablespoon onion, chopped
1 large garlic clove, finely
  chopped
1 tablespoon fresh parsley,
  chopped
1 slice of uncooked bacon
2 teaspoons vegetable oil
1 tablespoon tomato paste
¼ cup water
⅓ pound pasta
grated Parmesan cheese

Pasta and beans (fagioli) is a combination that allows for a lot of flexibility. Try different varieties of beans and different sizes and shapes of pasta in this recipe.

1. Soak the beans overnight in 4 cups water.

2. Next day, place the beans and the soaking water in a 3-quart stock pot. Season with ½ teaspoon salt. Bring to a rapid boil, then reduce the heat, cover and cook at a low boil until the beans are tender, about 1¾–2 hours.

3. Sauté the onion, garlic, parsley and bacon in vegetable oil until the onion is soft, about 1–2 minutes. Add the tomato paste and ¼ cup water, and cook on low for 3–5 minutes. Add to the bean mixture.

4. In a separate stock pot, bring 1½ quarts of lightly salted water to a boil. Add the pasta and cook until *al dente*, about 7 minutes. Pour off 1 to 3 cups of water, but do not drain completely. Add the bean mixture and simmer together for 5 minutes. Serve topped with grated Parmesan cheese.

gazpacho

SERVES 4
PREPARATION TIME:
45 MINUTES
PLUS 4 HOURS TO CHILL

1 cup chopped onions
1 cup chopped green peppers (2–3
   medium-size peppers)
4 garlic cloves, finely chopped
3 tablespoons fresh parsley,
   chopped
3 tablespoons vegetable oil
2–3 cucumbers, chopped (2 cups)
5–6 ripe red tomatoes (2 cups
   peeled and chopped)
6 ounces tomato paste
1 tablespoon vegetable oil
2 teaspoons vinegar
½ teaspoon salt
¼ teaspoon pepper
dash lemon juice
dash crushed red pepper
pinch sugar (to taste)

1. Sauté the onions, peppers, garlic, and parsley in the oil for about 5 minutes, just until the vegetables are a bit soft.

2. Combine the sautéed vegetables with the cucumbers and tomatoes in a blender. Process until well blended.

3. In a large bowl, combine the vegetables with the tomato paste, 1 tablespoon oil, and vinegar. Season with salt, pepper, lemon juice, crushed red pepper, and sugar. Refrigerate for at least 4 hours. Stir before serving.

cream of asparagus soup

SERVES 4–6
PREPARATION TIME:
50 MINUTES

3 cups chopped asparagus
½ cup chopped onion
1 garlic clove, chopped
1 chicken bouillon cube
1¼ teaspoons salt
⅛ teaspoon pepper
1½–2 cups milk
5–6 tablespoons flour
2 tablespoons butter
¼ cup heavy cream

1. Bring 2½ cups water (enough to cover the asparagus) to a boil. Add the asparagus, onion, garlic, bouillon cube, salt, and pepper. Simmer (covered) over medium to medium-high heat for 20–30 minutes, or until asparagus is tender.

2. Add 1¼ cup milk to the soup.

3. In a small bowl dissolve the flour in ¼ cup of the milk, blending carefully until all lumps disappear.

4. Pour the flour mixture into the soup. Cook for 4–5 minutes, stirring frequently while simmering. Additional milk may be added for a thinner soup. Add butter and heavy cream. Cook for 2–3 minutes longer uncovered. Serve hot.

Pasta

"Now bolt down these cloves of garlic. Well primed with garlic you will have greater mettle for the fight."

from KNIGHTS
Aristophanes

mostaccioli

rigatoni

ziti

vermicelli

fettucini

Garlic is used copiously to flavor a variety of sauces that accompany pasta. The preparation of basic tomato sauce begins with the sautéing of garlic and onions in vegetable or olive oil to create a flavorful base for the remaining ingredients. Finely chopped garlic combined with butter and parsley enhances the taste of cheese ravioli. Garlic is also used to season the meat fillings in ravioli and tortellini, and it makes an emphatic culinary contribution to clam and crab sauces served with spaghetti. Pesto, a zesty combination of garlic, basil, parsley and Parmesan cheese, is an excellent companion to pasta as well.

Pasta is good for us. It is not as fattening as one might think—only about 170 calories per 4-ounce serving, exclusive of any tomato or other sauce. Domestic pasta is usually made from fine, semolina durum wheat that is enriched with iron. It is a complex carbohydrate, containing little or no fat, yet rich in protein, vitamins, and minerals.

Pasta is available in a variety of shapes and sizes, which allows the cook to be imaginative and creative when serving meals that call for pasta. Some of the more common varieties are illustrated.

You will develop your own preferences for certain varieties of pastas in different dishes, but let me share with you some serving suggestions. When pasta is served as a main dish, topped with tomato sauce, I recommend a substantial pasta such as mafalde, mostaccioli, or rigatoni. Spaghetti or linguine with tomato sauce is a popular side dish to accompany a veal or chicken entrée.

Spaghetti is available in different thicknesses, and some commercial pasta companies assign numbers to the various thicknesses, generally numbers 8 to 11. Ordinarily, the larger the number, the finer, or

spaghetti

mafalde

farfalle (egg bows)

linguine

ditalini

pastina

thinner, the spaghetti. Thin spaghetti such as No. 11 is good in seafood dishes with clam or crab sauces, because the seafood sauces permeate and flavor the thin pasta varieties better.

Pastas that are well suited for soups include orzo, ditalini, and tubetini. There are some specialty shapes which are usually limited to specified meals: lasagna for the entrée of the same name, and large shells for stuffing with meat and cheese fillings. To ensure more thorough cooking, parboil lasagna and the large shells before using them in the recipe.

A number of domestic and imported brands of pasta are available on supermarket shelves. More exotic brands and more extensive varieties can be found in Italian specialty stores. There are a number of other ethnic pastas that are fun to try, especially a thin, Puerto Rican variety called fideos, which is excellent for soups. Another unusual pasta, which is available in Oriental food stores, is Japanese vermicelli—fine, almost transparent noodles made from potato starch.

Purists will argue that homemade pasta is far superior to any commercially prepared variety. For those of you who want to make your own pasta, I have included recipes for manicotti, tortellini, gnocchi, and ravioli. If you plan to make homemade pasta, a quality pasta machine is a good investment. It will considerably reduce the time you spend rolling out the dough. My machine is a manually operated (hand-cranked) model with rollers through which the dough is fed repeatedly until it attains the desired thinness. Other rollers cut the dough into fettucini or spaghetti shapes.

Prepared pasta should be cooked according to package directions, generally to the *al dente* stage (slightly firm to the bite). However, as with vegetables, you will determine your own preferences as to *al dente* or beyond. To cook 1 pound of spaghetti, use a 10–12-quart stockpot and bring at least 6 quarts of water (salt is optional) to a rapid boil. Add the pasta all at once and stir immediately with a long-handled fork to

lasagna

fusilli

shells

keep it from sticking together. A teaspoon of vegetable oil in the water will also keep the pasta from sticking. You may want to break the spaghetti in half for easier handling, but in any event, be sure it is completely submerged in the water. Cover the pot until the water returns to a boil, then remove the lid and allow the pasta to cook at a reduced but steady boil. Stir frequently. Test the pasta after 5 minutes and then every minute or so until the desired cooked stage is attained. (Homemade pasta takes considerably less time to cook than commercially prepared pasta.) Drain, top with sauce, and serve immediately.

mom's tomato sauce and meatballs

MAKES 1 QUART (4
SERVINGS)
PREPARATION TIME:
1½–2 HOURS PLUS 2½
HOURS TO SIMMER

½ **pound pork neck bones or**
   spareribs
4–5 **tablespoons vegetable oil**
1 **tablespoon olive oil**
2 **garlic cloves, finely chopped**
½ **cup chopped onion**
3 **tablespoons fresh parsley,**
   chopped
½ **cup lean ground beef**
5–6 **fennel seeds**
6 **ounces tomato paste**
½ **teaspoon salt**
⅛ **teaspoon pepper**
4–5 **basil leaves**
28 **ounces tomato purée**
⅛ **teaspoon oregano**
1 **tablespoon sugar (to taste)**
½ **pound sweet Italian sausage,**
   cut into 3-inch links

When my mother makes this sauce, she starts with the tomato purée that she has canned using garden-fresh plum tomatoes. If you don't can your own tomatoes, experiment with different commercial brands until you find the quality and flavor you like best.

1. Rinse the neck bones in cold water. Drain and pat dry. In a large stockpot, brown them in 2–3 tablespoons oil over medium to medium-high heat for 10–15 minutes. Remove the meat from the pan and set aside.

2. Sauté the garlic, onion, and parsley in the stockpot. Add a little more oil if needed. When the onion is soft, add the ground beef and season with fennel seeds. Cook until browned, about 5 minutes. Add the tomato paste and simmer for 5 minutes, stirring often. Season with salt, pepper, and basil leaves. Fill the empty tomato paste can with water (about ¾ cup) and add to the stockpot. Cover and simmer for 7–10 minutes.

3. Add the tomato purée and 3–4 cups water. Season with the oregano and sugar to taste. Allow the tomato sauce to come to a soft boil, then lower to simmer. Cook for 1 hour, stirring often.

4. Brown the sausage in a separate pan. Drain. Add the sausage together with the neck bones and meatballs (see below) to the tomato sauce. Continue to simmer for 1½ hours more, with the lid ajar. Stir frequently, adding more water if necessary.

Meatballs:

1 slice day-old Italian bread
⅛–¼ cup milk
½ pound ground beef, pork, and
   veal
1–2 eggs, beaten
½ teaspoon salt
dash pepper
1 small garlic clove, finely
   chopped
1½ tablespoons grated Parmesan
   cheese
1½ teaspoons fresh parsley,
   chopped
breadcrumbs (optional)
3–6 tablespoons vegetable oil

1. Soak the bread in the milk, squeeze out excess milk, and crumble the bread into loose pieces.

2. Mix the bread with the meat, eggs, salt, pepper, garlic, cheese, and parsley. Shape the mixture into balls, adding some breadcrumbs if the mixture seems too soft.

3. Brown the meatballs in the vegetable oil for 7–10 minutes and then add them to the tomato sauce along with the sausage and neck bones. Drain all but 1–2 tablespoons oil and meat drippings from the frying pan. Add ¼ cup water and allow the meat drippings and water to simmer together for 1–2 minutes. Add to the tomato sauce.

maureen's tomato sauce

MAKES 1 QUART (4
SERVINGS)
PREPARATION TIME:
30 MINUTES PLUS 2–3 HOURS
TO SIMMER

Use large Italian plum tomatoes, if possible. The solid pulp of these tomatoes makes a thick sauce. To remove the tomato skins, pour boiling water over the tomatoes and let them soak for 3–5 minutes, then submerge them in cold water. The skins will slip off easily.

This sauce can be kept in the refrigerator for up to a week or in a plastic container in the freezer for two months.

½ cup chopped red or green
   sweet peppers
½ cup chopped carrot
½ cup chopped onion
½ cup chopped celery
3 garlic cloves, finely chopped
1 tablespoon fresh parsley, finely
   chopped
2 tablespoons olive oil
1 tablespoon butter
1 tablespoon brown sugar
3 pounds ripe red tomatoes,
   peeled and chopped
1 cup chicken stock
1 teaspoon paprika
2 teaspoons salt
¼ teaspoon pepper
2 bay leaves
½ clove, crushed

1. In a large skillet, sauté the peppers, carrot, onion, celery, garlic, and parsley in oil and butter, for about 12 minutes over low to medium heat. Then add the brown sugar. When the sugar is dissolved, transfer the sautéed vegetables to a blender and purée them.

2. Transfer the puréed vegetables to a 3-quart saucepan. Add the tomatoes, chicken stock, and remaining seasonings. Bring the sauce to a boil, then lower to simmer, and cook with the lid ajar for 2–3 hours, until thickened, stirring occasionally. Remove the bay leaves before serving.

gnocchi

SERVES 4–6
PREPARATION TIME:
1½–2 HOURS

2 cups ricotta cheese
2 cups flour
dash salt (about ⅛ teaspoon)
1 quart Mom's Tomato Sauce
    (page 82)
grated Parmesan cheese

In most recipes for gnocchi, potatoes are the primary ingredient, but here ricotta cheese is featured instead. These gnocchi are so rich, you can enjoy them as a main entrée, complemented with a salad or other green vegetable.

1. Knead together the ricotta, flour, and salt until the dough is smooth. Set aside to rest for 15 minutes. Then roll out the dough on a floured board to a rectangular shape about ¼-inch thick. Cut into ½-inch strips. Roll to stretch into pencil-size thickness. Cut all strips crosswise into ½-inch pieces. On a floured board, press down on each piece of dough with your floured thumb, drawing the dough toward you so that it forms into a curled shape. (If you are not going to use the gnocchi immediately, place them on a cookie sheet and freeze for about ½ hour, then store in a plastic bag in the freezer.)

2. Cook the gnocchi for 20–25 minutes in 6 quarts rapidly boiling lightly salted water. Drain. Serve topped with tomato sauce and grated cheese.

ravioli della nonna braida

MAKES ABOUT 250 RAVIOLI
PREPARATION TIME:
3½–4 HOURS PLUS 3 HOURS
TO BAKE THE ROAST

This recipe is designed for those who want to make one large batch of ravioli which can be frozen and used for several meals. (Six to eight ravioli makes one serving.)

Note: A meat grinder, a pasta machine, and a ravioli cutter are necessary for this recipe.

1 6-pound boneless chuck roast
1 stalk celery
8–10 onion slices
3 teaspoons salt
10 ounces frozen, chopped
    spinach
¾–1 cup chopped onion
2 large garlic cloves, finely
    chopped
3–4 tablespoons vegetable oil
1 cup fresh parsley, chopped
¾ teaspoon salt
1¼ teaspoons allspice
¾ teaspoon cinnamon
3 pounds ricotta cheese
6 eggs, beaten
½ teaspoon salt

1. Preheat the oven to 400°F. Place the meat in the roasting pan. Add the celery and scatter the onion slices over the roast. Season with 3 teaspoons salt. (Do not add water.) Cover and cook in the oven for 30 minutes; then lower the oven temperature to 350°F. and bake for about 2½ hours longer.

2. Cut the cooked roast into strips. When cool enough to handle, feed the roast through a meat grinder until a fine consistency is attained.

3. Heat the spinach in a small amount of water. Drain.

4. In a skillet, sauté the onion and garlic in 3–4 tablespoons vegetable oil for about 10 minutes, until the onion is soft.

5. Combine the ground meat, onion, garlic, spinach, and parsley. Season with ¾ teaspoon salt, the allspice and cinnamon. Stir well. Refrigerate for about 15 minutes.

6. Mix the ricotta cheese with the eggs and ½ teaspoon salt. Add to the meat mixture and set aside while you make the pasta.

7. For ease of handling, mix half the pasta ingredients at a time. Combine 8 beaten eggs and 2¾ tablespoons oil with ¾ cup warm

16 cups flour
16 eggs
5½ tablespoons vegetable oil
1¾–2 cups warm water

water. Make a well in the center of 8 cups flour. Add the liquids to the flour and stir in the flour gradually until all the ingredients are combined. Turn the dough out onto a lightly floured surface. Knead for 5–8 minutes. If the dough is sticky, add more flour, a little at a time, until the dough is smooth. If the dough is too stiff, add water, a tablespoon at a time, until the texture of the dough is smooth. (With practice you will get a feel for making pasta dough.)

8. When you have mixed all the dough, shape it into two large balls. Coat the balls lightly with vegetable oil, cover them, and allow the dough to rest for 10 minutes. Cut the dough into pieces small enough to feed into the pasta machine (about 2 by 4 inches). Dust each piece lightly with flour. Feed the dough through the rollers on the pasta machine, through settings 1–5, to form long, thin, rectangular strips, 3–4 inches wide and 1½–2 feet long. Dot half of each strip with tablespoon-size portions of filling. The finished ravioli will be about 2 inches square, so space the filling accordingly. Fold the other half of the dough over the filling. Press to seal the edges. Cut with a ravioli cutter. Cook the ravioli fresh or freeze them for 30 minutes on lightly floured cookie sheets, then transfer to plastic bags for long-term (two months) freezer storage.

9. To cook, add the ravioli to rapidly boiling salted water and boil for 8–10 minutes, or until the sealed edges of the dough are tender. Serve topped with tomato sauce (from Mom's Tomato Sauce and Meatballs, page 82), pesto (from Pesto Linguine, page 95) or butter, garlic, and parsley.

ravioli with garlic butter

SERVES 2
PREPARATION TIME:
30 MINUTES

12 large frozen cheese ravioli
2–3 tablespoons butter, melted
1 garlic clove, finely chopped
2–3 tablespoons fresh parsley,
chopped
2 tablespoons grated Parmesan
cheese
1–2 tablespoons vegetable oil
1–2 tablespoons water

For a quick pasta dinner, select a variety of packaged frozen ravioli filled with ricotta cheese and seasoned with Romano cheese, parsley, salt, and pepper. Avoid brands using bulk fillers, preservatives, or artificial flavors.

1. Cook the ravioli according to package directions until the dough is tender, 10–15 minutes.

2. Meanwhile, combine all the remaining ingredients. Drain the ravioli quickly. Pour the sauce over it, toss and serve immediately.

lasagna

SERVES 8–10
PREPARATION TIME:
1½ HOURS

Lasagna can be prepared ahead of time, refrigerated overnight or frozen for 1 or 2 weeks, and then reheated — you may want to add more tomato sauce at serving time.

2 teaspoons vegetable oil
1 pound lasagna noodles
¼ cup chopped onion
1 garlic clove, finely chopped
1 teaspoon salt (optional)
dash pepper
1 pound lean ground chuck
1–2 tablespoons vegetable oil
½–1 pound sweet Italian sausage
1½ quarts tomato sauce (from Mom's Tomato Sauce and Meatballs, page 82)
1 pound ricotta cheese
2 eggs, beaten
2–3 tablespoons fresh parsley, chopped
2 tablespoons grated Parmesan cheese (plus some to sprinkle on each layer)
salt and pepper to taste
8 ounces grated mozzarella cheese

1. Add 2 teaspoons vegetable oil to 6 quarts lightly salted water and bring it to a rapid boil. Add the lasagna and cook for 8–10 minutes. Drain. Pour cold water over the lasagna. Drain again.

2. Sauté the onion and garlic in 2 tablespoons vegetable oil. Add the ground chuck and cook until browned. Season with salt (optional) and pepper. Remove from the pan. Remove the sausage from its casing and brown it for 10–15 minutes. Discard any excess fat. Combine the tomato sauce, sausage, and ground beef, and simmer for 10 minutes.

3. Mix the ricotta with the eggs, parsley, Parmesan cheese, pepper, and salt. Preheat the oven to 350°F

4. In a 9″ × 13″ baking dish, layer the lasagna alternately with the ricotta mixture, mozzarella, tomato sauce, and additional Parmesan cheese. Begin and end the layering with tomato sauce. Any extra tomato sauce may be used when serving. Cover the dish with foil and bake for 40 minutes or until thoroughly heated. If the lasagna appears watery, remove the foil for the last 10 minutes. Serve.

stuffed shells

SERVES 8–10
PREPARATION TIME:
75 MINUTES

Two types of aged, grated cheese are suggested as alternate ingredients for this recipe. One is Parmesan, a mild flavored, universally popular, and commonly available cheese. The other, locatelli, has a zestier taste and is available primarily in Italian specialty food shops. Purchase either one in a block and grate it just before it's needed.

1 pound large (2–3-inch)
  macaroni shells
1 garlic clove, finely chopped
¼ cup chopped onion
2 tablespoons vegetable oil
1 pound ground chuck
1 teaspoon salt
1 tablespoon fresh parsley, chopped
dash pepper
2 pounds ricotta cheese
3 eggs, beaten
½ cup grated mozzarella cheese
3 tablespoons grated locatelli or
  Parmesan cheese (plus some
  to sprinkle on top)
3 tablespoons fresh parsley,
  chopped
½–1 quart tomato sauce (from
  Mom's Tomato Sauce and
  Meatballs, page 82)

1. Add the macaroni shells to 6 quarts lightly salted boiling water. When the water returns to a boil, lower the heat to medium-high and cook the shells for 12–15 minutes. Do not overcook. Drain. Pour cold water over the macaroni, and drain again.

2. Sauté the garlic and onion in vegetable oil for 3–4 minutes. Add the ground beef. Season with the 1 teaspoon salt, 1 tablespoon parsley, and pepper, and cook until the beef is browned. Drain off any excess oil. Allow the meat to cool.

3. Combine the ricotta, eggs, mozzarella cheese, grated locatelli or Parmesan, parsley, and ground meat.

4. Preheat the oven to 350°F. Stuff the shells with the filling and place them in a baking dish. Top with tomato sauce and more grated cheese. Cover the dish with foil and bake for 25–30 minutes. Serve.

manicotti

SERVES 8–10
PREPARATION TIME:
1¾ HOURS

7 eggs
¾–1 teaspoon salt
1¾ cups flour
1¾ cups water
filling for Stuffed Shells, page 90
1–1½ quarts tomato sauce (from Mom's Tomato Sauce and Meatballs, page 82)

Manicotti pasta is large and tubular shaped, designed to be filled. I recommend the flavor of this homemade, crêpe-like pasta, which is lighter and more delicate than the commercially prepared product. This recipe makes 24 pieces. The filling for this pasta is the same as the filling for Stuffed Shells.

1. Preheat oven to 350°F.

2. Beat the eggs and season with the salt. Add the flour alternately with the water. Mix until the batter is smooth. It will be very thin.

3. Lightly season a 6-inch iron skillet by using a paper towel to spread a couple of drops of vegetable oil around the inside. Then heat the pan over medium to medium-high heat. When the pan is hot, spoon in enough batter to thinly coat the bottom of the skillet. The batter will cook very quickly (20–30 seconds). Cook on one side only, just until the top side looks cooked. Slide the finished crêpe out onto a dishtowel to cool. Lightly grease the pan again before each crêpe.

4. When all the crêpes are cooked, place about ¼ cup of filling on each and roll into a cylinder. Pour enough tomato sauce into a baking dish to cover the bottom. Place the manicotti in the baking dish with the overlapping ends underneath. Pour the remaining tomato sauce over the manicotti. Cover the dish with aluminum foil. Bake in the oven for 30 minutes. Serve.

tortellini

Select prime veal and pork cubes, then ask your butcher to grind the meat twice so that it will have a fine consistency. I enjoy these tortellini served in a chicken broth such as the one in the recipe for Escarole Soup on page 66. You can also top them with tomato sauce or smother them in a cream sauce. I recommend a pasta machine for rolling out the dough.

This recipe will make 325–350 tortellini. You can divide them into four 1-pound packages and freeze for later use. Each 1-pound package will serve 4–6.

Filling:

½ **pound ground pork**
½ **pound ground veal**
2 **eggs, beaten**
1 **teaspoon fresh parsley, chopped**
1¼ **teaspoons nutmeg**
½ **cup plus 2 tablespoons grated Parmesan or locatelli cheese**
½ **teaspoon salt**
1 **garlic clove, finely chopped**
1 **tablespoon breadcrumbs**

1. Mix all the ingredients for the filling and set aside.

2. Make a well in the center of the flour. Beat together the eggs, oil, water, and salt and pour into the well. Form a dough by slowly incorporating the flour into the liquid ingredients, adding 1–2 tablespoons more water if the dough is too dry. Turn the dough onto a lightly floured board and knead it for about 10 minutes. The dough should be fairly stiff. Cover the dough and allow it to rest for 10–15 minutes.

3. Cut the dough into pieces about 2 by 4 inches and feed them through all settings of the rollers on a pasta machine.

Pasta:

5 cups flour
5 eggs
1 tablespoon vegetable oil
8 tablespoons warm water
1 teaspoon salt (optional)

4. Cut the rolled-out dough into 2-inch squares. Dot each square with ½ teaspoon filling. Fold each square into a triangle shape and press to seal all edges. Twist each triangle around your index finger to join the two opposite corners of the triangle. (If you are not going to serve them right away, place the tortellini on cookie sheets and freeze for 1 hour until frozen hard, then store in plastic bags and freeze for future use.)

5. To cook, drop the tortellini into boiling water, or Tortellini Broth (page 73) and boil for 25–30 minutes if frozen, or 10–15 minutes if fresh. Serve with tomato sauce (from Mom's Tomato Sauce and Meatballs, page 82).

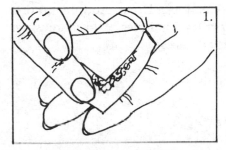
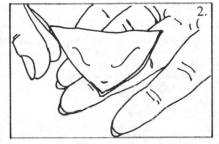

spinach fettucini royale

SERVES 4
PREPARATION TIME:
50–60 MINUTES

Green spinach fettucini, commonly available in most supermarkets, is richer in iron and potassium than most other pasta varieties. For the ground meat in this recipe, I suggest a blend of pork, veal, and beef, which can be purchased from your supermarket or butcher.

¼ cup chopped onion
1 large garlic clove, chopped
1 tablespoon fresh parsley,
  chopped
2 tablespoons oil
2 tablespoons butter
½ pound ground pork, veal, and
  beef
1 teaspoon salt
⅛ teaspoon pepper
3–4 tablespoons tomato paste
¼–½ cup water
½ pound spinach fettucini
grated Parmesan cheese

1. Sauté the onion, garlic, and parsley in oil and butter. Add the ground meat and cook until it loses its pink color. Season with salt and pepper.

2. Add the tomato paste and mix well. Add ¼ cup water. Cook for 15 minutes. If too dry, add another ¼ cup water.

3. Meanwhile, bring 3 quarts lightly salted water to a boil. Add the pasta and cook until tender (7–10 minutes). Drain. Add the ground beef mixture. Mix well and simmer for 5 minutes. Add more water if too dry. Serve topped with grated cheese.

pesto linguine

SERVES 4
PREPARATION TIME:
45 MINUTES

Pesto sauce features the enticingly aromatic flavor of sweet basil, highlighted by the pungent taste of garlic. Good-quality virgin olive oil is the medium that blends these flavors with the zest of parsley and the delightfully nutty flavor of freshly grated Parmesan cheese.

This recipe makes about 1½ cups. The extra sauce can be stored in the refrigerator for two or three weeks or in the freezer for two months. Be sure that the basil leaves and parsley are submerged in the oil. Warm to room temperature before using.

5 large garlic cloves
1 packed cup fresh parsley, tough stems removed
1 packed cup basil leaves, tough stems removed
1 cup olive oil
½ cup grated, good-quality domestic or imported Parmesan cheese
1 pound thin linguine
4–6 tablespoons butter

1. Place the garlic, parsley, and basil in a blender and mix until all the ingredients are finely chopped. Then add the oil and blend for 10–20 seconds. Add the grated cheese and blend for 10–15 seconds longer.

2. Cook the linguine to the *al dente* stage in rapidly boiling, lightly salted water, according to package instructions. Drain.

3. Add the butter to the hot linguine. Mix in 4–8 tablespoons pesto sauce. If too dry, add a few tablespoons of warm water and/or a few drops of olive oil. Top with additional grated cheese and serve immediately.

zucchini and pasta

SERVES 3–4
PREPARATION TIME:
30–45 MINUTES

2–3 garlic cloves, finely chopped
⅓ cup sliced onion
3 tablespoons vegetable oil
3–4 tablespoons butter
1 medium-size zucchini, sliced,
  unpeeled (3 cups)
¼–½ teaspoon salt
⅛ teaspoon pepper
¼ pound thin spaghetti (No. 8)
grated Parmesan cheese

Zucchini is available fresh in your local supermarket almost year round. Select firm, bright green zucchini.

1. Sauté the garlic and onion in oil and half of the butter until tender. Add the zucchini and season with salt and pepper. Add the remaining butter and sauté (covered) for 10 minutes, or until the zucchini is tender but not overcooked. Stir occasionally.

2. Cook the spaghetti in rapidly boiling lightly salted water for 7–10 minutes. Drain. Add the zucchini, top with grated cheese, and serve.

cauliflower and pasta

SERVES 4
PREPARATION TIME:
35–45 MINUTES

3 garlic cloves, finely chopped
2–3 tablespoons fresh parsley,
  chopped
2 tablespoons olive oil
2 tablespoons vegetable oil
2 cups cauliflower, cut into small
  pieces
¼ cup water
salt and pepper to taste
1 cup spinach pasta twists
grated Parmesan or Romano
  cheese

Cauliflower is available fresh in your local supermarket almost year round. Select bright, white compact heads. Any green leaves surrounding the heads should look crisp.

1. Sauté the garlic and parsley in both oils for 1–3 minutes.

2. Add the cauliflower and water and steam for about 5 minutes, until tender. Add more water, as necessary. Season with salt and pepper. Do not overcook.

3. Boil the pasta in lightly salted water until cooked (about 7 minutes). Drain. Add to the cauliflower. Top with grated cheese and serve hot.

clams and spaghetti

SERVES 3–4
PREPARATION TIME:
45 MINUTES

4 garlic cloves, finely chopped
⅓ heaping cup fresh parsley,
  chopped
5 tablespoons vegetable oil
2 tablespoons olive oil
¼ teaspoon salt
⅛ teaspoon pepper
½ cup water
2 6½-ounce cans minced clams
½ pound spaghetti (No. 11)
grated Parmesan or locatelli
  cheese

Very thin spaghetti or linguine tastes best in this entrée because the clam sauce can easily permeate and flavor the thin pasta. I suggest using canned minced clams in the sauce, since fresh, whole clams can sometimes be tough.

1. Sauté the garlic and parsley for 1–2 minutes in both oils. Season with salt and pepper. Add ½ cup water and the juice in which the clams are packed. Bring to a hard boil, and then add the minced clams. Allow the clams to heat through, but remove the pan from the heat just before the sauce returns to a boil, or the clams may become tough. Cover, and keep hot.

2. Meanwhile, cook the spaghetti in rapidly boiling, lightly salted water for about 7 minutes, to the *al dente* stage. Drain. Add the clam sauce. Serve topped with Parmesan cheese.

crab and spaghetti

SERVES 3–4
PREPARATION TIME:
45–60 MINUTES

Live, hard-shelled crabs are available in coastal areas where they are harvested. In the Middle Atlantic states, crabs are abundantly available in July and August. They are highly perishable and for that reason are seldom shipped any great distance. Select crabs that are alive and show signs of movement and use them the same day you purchase them.

Serve this dish with a generous supply of paper towels—it's wonderfully messy. I recommend eating the spaghetti out from under the crabs before it gets cold.

2 dozen medium-size blue-point
   crabs, cleaned
1 teaspoon salt
½ cup parsley, chopped
½ teaspoon oregano
4 garlic cloves, chopped
½ cup oil
4 tablespoons vinegar
1–2 cups water
½ pound spaghetti (No. 10)
grated Parmesan, Romano, or
   locatelli cheese

1. Separate the claws from the crab bodies. Place the crabs in a large pot over high heat. Season with salt, parsley, oregano, garlic, oil, and vinegar. Add the water and steam the crabs until they turn red (about 20 minutes). Gently toss the crabs several times to blend all flavorings. Add more water as needed.

2. Meanwhile, cook the spaghetti in boiling, lightly salted water for about 7 minutes. Do not overcook. Drain. Top with the crabs, crab juice, and grated cheese, and serve immediately.

pasta with tuna sauce

SERVES 4
PREPARATION TIME:
30–45 MINUTES

2 garlic cloves, chopped
1 tablespoon vegetable oil
2 tablespoons olive oil
7 ounces white tuna (packed in
    water, drained)
6 ounces tomato paste
1–1¼ cups water
2 tablespoons fresh parsley,
    chopped
¼ teaspoon oregano
salt and pepper to taste
pinch sugar
½ pound spaghetti
grated Parmesan cheese

Canned tuna is available as white meat or red meat, packed in water or oil. Tuna packed in water contains fewer calories than tuna packed in oil. I find that white tuna packed in water has a mild flavor, very suitable for this sauce.

1. Sauté the garlic in both oils for 30–60 seconds. Add the tuna, tomato paste, and water. Season with parsley, oregano, salt and pepper, and sugar. Simmer for 10–15 minutes.

2. Cook the spaghetti in lightly salted water according to package instructions. Drain. Top with the sauce and grated cheese. Serve hot.

Main-dish Vegetables

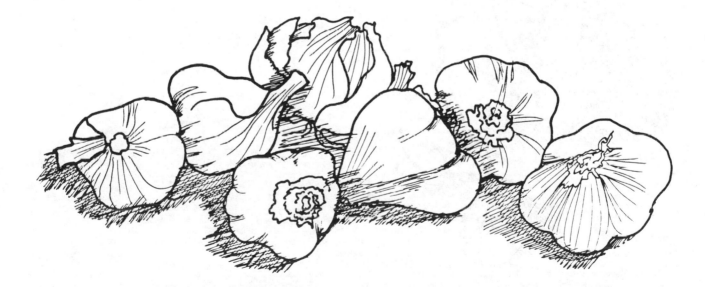

> "Sith garlic then hath poure to save from death
>   Bear with it though it make unsavoure breathe."

—Robert of Normandy (1100 A.D.)

Vegetables needn't be restricted to supporting roles in your meal planning. Why not give them the break they deserve and allow them to star in your meal preparation? The recipes presented in this chapter suggest delicious ways of doing just that. The addition of garlic adds a special flavor emphasis to the award-winning taste of eggplant, zucchini, peppers, and other vegetables.

Combined with grated Parmesan cheese and parsley, garlic perks up the stuffing in Stuffed Long Sweet Peppers. The meat fillings in Eggplant Oven Sandwiches and in Stuffed Bell Peppers benefit from its flavorfulness, and a special blend of cinnamon, allspice, and garlic in Stuffed Italian Long Neck Squash gives the ground meat filling a delicious, extraordinary taste. Garlic also highlights the flavor of the two vegetarian stews of eggplant and zucchini, and delicately seasons Stuffed Cabbage, a traditional Polish dish.

eggplant parmesan

SERVES 8–10
PREPARATION TIME:
1½–2 HOURS

Look for egglants with shiny bright skins, deep purple, almost black in color. They should be solid and firm to the touch. Choose small or medium-size eggplants—they are more likely to be tender and sweet tasting.

3 eggplants (about 4 pounds)
flour
vegetable oil
2 garlic cloves, finely chopped
¼ cup chopped onion
3 tablespoons oil
2–3 tablespoons fresh parsley,
   chopped
6–8 ounces ground chuck
salt and pepper to taste
24 ounces tomato sauce
15–16 ounces ricotta cheese
2 eggs, beaten
8 ounces grated mozzarella cheese
   (about 2 cups)
¼ cup grated Parmesan cheese
12 fresh basil leaves

1. Peel the eggplant and discard the ends. Slice crosswise into ⅜-inch-thick slices. Dust with flour.

2. In a large skillet, heat enough vegetable oil to cover the bottom of the pan. When it is hot, fry the eggplant slices over medium-high to high heat until soft and light brown in color. Add more oil as needed. Drain on paper towels.

3. Meanwhile, sauté the garlic and onion in 3 tablespoons oil for 3–5 minutes, or until the onion is soft. Add the parsley and ground chuck. Sauté until the meat is browned. Lightly season the ground meat with salt and pepper to taste. Drain off any excess oil. Add the tomato sauce. Simmer on low for about 30 minutes. Stir occasionally. Add some water, if needed. Combine the ricotta cheese and eggs. Preheat the oven to 400°F.

4. In a large baking dish, place the eggplant, cheeses, basil leaves, and tomato sauce in alternate layers until all ingredients are used. Start and finish the layers with tomato sauce. Cover the dish loosely with aluminum foil. Bake for 30 minutes, until the tomato sauce bubbles and the eggplant is thoroughly heated. If, after 20 minutes, the tomato sauce is watery, remove the aluminum foil and bake for 10 more minutes uncovered. Serve immediately.

eggplant stew

SERVES 4
PREPARATION TIME:
60 MINUTES

Plum tomatoes are suggested for this recipe. They are somewhat oblong shaped, 2 to 4 inches in length. These tomatoes have a thick pulp and little juice, and for that reason they are favored for making tomato paste, tomato sauce, and stews.

1 small eggplant (1 pound)
¼ cup vegetable oil
2 tablespoons chopped onion
1 medium-size garlic clove,
 chopped
3 basil leaves
2 tablespoons fresh parsley,
 chopped
4 plum tomatoes, peeled and
 sliced (about 1 heaping cup)
1 teaspoon salt
⅛ teaspoon pepper
¼ teaspoon oregano
1 teaspoon sugar

1. Cut the eggplant into cubes; do not peel. Place in a 3-quart sauce-pan with the oil, onion, garlic, basil, and parsley. Mix well to completely coat the eggplant lightly with oil. Cook over high heat, stirring often to brown the eggplant (about 7 minutes).

2. Add the tomatoes and season with salt, pepper, oregano, and sugar. Cover the pot, reduce the heat to low, and cook until the eggplant is tender (15–20 minutes). Stir often. Serve hot.

eggplant oven sandwiches

SERVES 6–8
PREPARATION TIME:
60 MINUTES

2 tablespoons chopped onions
1 tablespoon vegetable oil
8 ounces tomato sauce
salt and pepper to taste
2–3 medium-size eggplants
2–3 slices day-old bread
¼ cup milk
¾ pound ground beef
2 garlic cloves, chopped
1 tablespoon chopped onion
1½ tablespoons fresh parsley,
   chopped
2 eggs, beaten
2 heaping tablespoons ricotta
   cheese
½ teaspoon salt
⅛ teaspoon pepper
2–3 teaspoons grated Parmesan
   cheese, plus extra for topping
vegetable oil

1. Preheat the oven to 400°F.

2. Start the sauce by sautéing the onion in oil. Add the tomato sauce. Season with salt and pepper. Simmer for 5–10 minutes.

3. Meanwhile, peel and slice the eggplants into ¼–⅜-inch slices. Soak the bread in the milk, squeeze it dry and crumble it into small pieces. Mix all the remaining ingredients, except the vegetable oil, with the bread. Shape the mixture into patties and place between two slices of eggplant.

4. Coat the outsides of the eggplant sandwiches lightly with the oil. Place on a greased cookie sheet.

5. Bake in the oven for about 10 minutes on each side, until the eggplant is tender and lightly browned. Add more oil if necessary. Remove from the oven and lower the oven temperature to 350°F. Drain on paper towels. Then return the eggplant sandwiches to the cookie sheet. Pour the tomato sauce over them. Bake another 10–15 minutes at 350°F. Top with grated cheese and serve.

stuffed long sweet peppers

SERVES 6
PREPARATION TIME:
1½ HOURS

As peppers mature, they turn from green to red. Look for peppers with some red coloring—they seem to be sweeter—and select only those that are firm to the touch. They can sometimes be found at roadside farmers' markets in mid-summer.

The peppers in this recipe can be stuffed a day ahead and refrigerated until you are ready to bake them.

20 long sweet peppers
4–5 tablespoons chopped onion
4 garlic cloves, finely chopped
2 tablespoons butter
1–2 teaspoons vegetable oil
1 cup breadcrumbs
2 large eggs, beaten
2 tablespoons fresh parsley, chopped
3 tablespoons grated Parmesan cheese
5 tablespoons milk
¾ cup ground chuck (6–8 ounces)
¼ teaspoon salt
⅛–¼ teaspoon pepper
4–5 tablespoons vegetable oil

1. Rinse and dry the peppers and remove the stem ends and seeds. Make one lengthwise cut in each pepper, stopping halfway to the tip.

2. Sauté the onion and garlic in butter and vegetable oil until the onion is tender, 3–4 minutes. Then add the remaining ingredients, except the vegetable oil. If the mixture is too moist, add more breadcrumbs.

3. Preheat the oven to 375°F. Spoon the stuffing into the peppers. Place the stuffed peppers in a roasting pan and coat them with a thin film of vegetable oil. Bake uncovered for 50–60 minutes, turning occasionally. The skin of the peppers should be soft when tested with a fork. Serve.

stuffed bell peppers

SERVES 6–8
PREPARATION TIME:
1½ HOURS

Choose firm, dark green peppers known as "bell," or "bullnose," peppers, or try a lighter green, thin-walled pepper with a tapered shape, sometimes referred to as a "cubanelle." Bell peppers are commonly available in supermarkets year round. The other variety is more likely to be available at farmers' markets in middle to late summer.

1 cup uncooked rice
11–12 bell peppers
1 pound lean ground chuck (or
    ground beef, veal, and pork)
1 teaspoon salt
½ teaspoon pepper
¼ cup grated Parmesan cheese
2 eggs, beaten
2–3 tablespoons fresh parsley,
    chopped
¼ cup chopped onion
1 garlic clove, finely chopped
5–6 tablespoons vegetable oil
16 ounces tomato sauce
1–1½ cups water
2 tablespoons sugar

1. Cook the rice in lightly salted water, according to package directions. When it is cooked, allow it to cool slightly.

2. Wash the peppers and remove the stem ends and seeds. Drain and pat dry.

3. Preheat the oven to 450°F. Combine the ground meat, salt and pepper, cheese, eggs, parsley, onion, and garlic with the cooked rice. Stuff the peppers with this mixture.

4. Place the stuffed peppers in a roasting pan. Pour vegetable oil over them. Roast the peppers in the oven for 20 minutes, turning often to brown all sides. Remove from the oven and reduce the oven temperature to 350°F.

5. Combine the tomato sauce, water, and sugar. Pour over the peppers. Cover the pan and bake for 30–40 minutes or longer, until the peppers are soft and tender. Turn occasionally. Add additional water if the sauce dries up too much. Serve.

zucchini stew

SERVES 4–6
PREPARATION TIME:
45–60 MINUTES

2 medium-size zucchini, sliced
　　into thick slices (about 1
　　pound)
1 medium-size onion, sliced (½
　　cup)
2 garlic cloves, chopped
2 cups peeled and sliced tomatoes
4 small potatoes, peeled and
　　sliced
½ green pepper, sliced
1 teaspoon salt
¼ teaspoon pepper
½ teaspoon oregano
2 teaspoons fresh parsley,
　　chopped
2 basil leaves, chopped (about ½
　　teaspoon)
½ teaspoon sugar
2 tablespoons vegetable oil

1. Place all the ingredients in a 3-quart saucepan. Stir to blend. Cover with a lid and cook over high heat, stirring often, for 3–5 minutes, sufficient time to form some juices.
2. Lower the heat to medium-high and cook for 20–25 more minutes. Stir periodically. The stew is cooked when the potatoes are tender. Serve.

stuffed italian long-neck squash

SERVES 6
PREPARATION TIME:
1½–1¾ HOURS

Long-neck squash is yellowish green, 2–3 feet long and about 3 inches in diameter at maturity. Since it generally grows in a curved shape, it is sometimes called "crooked-neck" squash. It is available in August, but probably only from a farmer's produce stand. If you cannot locate this variety of squash, use zucchini in this recipe.

You can prepare the squash ahead of time by following the first three steps of the recipe and then refrigerating it until the following day, when you finish by simmering the squash in the tomato sauce.

2–3 long-neck squash or 4–5
  zucchini (enough to make 12
  pieces, 3 inches long)
4–5 tablespoons vegetable oil
¼ cup sliced onions

Filling:
5–6 slices stale bread
½ cup milk
1¼ pounds ground chuck
2 garlic cloves, finely chopped
¼ cup chopped onions
1½ teaspoons cinnamon

1. Remove the skin of the squash, using a sharp knife or vegetable peeler. Cut off the ends of the squash and discard. Cut the squash into 3–4-inch segments. Scoop out the seeds and leave about ½ inch of pulp inside the squash.

2. Preheat the oven to 450°F. Moisten the bread in the milk, squeeze out any excess milk, and crumble the bread into loose pieces (about 1 cup, moistened and packed). Combine with the remaining filling ingredients. If too soft, add some breadcrumbs. Stuff the squash segments, and place them in a large baking dish. Top with sliced onions. Pour 4–5 tablespoons vegetable oil over the squash. Coat all surfaces of the squash lightly with oil. Roast in the oven until tender and lightly browned, 25–30 minutes.

1 teaspoon allspice
2 tablespoons fresh parsley, chopped
1–2 tablespoons fresh basil, chopped
3 eggs, beaten
1½ teaspoons salt
½ teaspoon pepper
breadcrumbs (optional)

Sauce:

2 tablespoons chopped onion
1 garlic clove, finely chopped
2–3 tablespoons vegetable oil
16 ounces tomato sauce
16 ounces water
2–3 basil leaves
salt and pepper to taste

3. While the squash is browning, prepare the sauce. Sauté the onion and garlic in vegetable oil for 2–3 minutes. Add the tomato sauce and an equal amount of water (use the empty tomato sauce can to measure the water). Add the basil leaves and salt and pepper. Allow the tomato sauce to simmer slowly over low heat for 10–15 minutes.

4. Remove the squash from the baking dish and place it in a dutch oven. Pour the tomato sauce over the squash, covering it completely. Add the drippings from the baking dish in which the squash was browned. Cover the dutch oven with a lid and simmer for about 30 minutes, or until the squash is very tender and the meat is cooked. Serve.

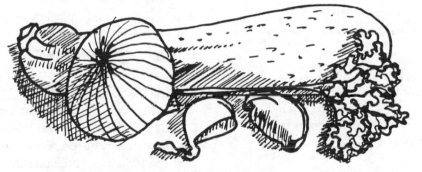

stuffed cabbage

SERVES 8
PREPARATION TIME:
1½–2 HOURS

Select a green head of cabbage with little or no white coloring. Older, tough cabbage has lost most of its green color. This recipe is good for using up leftover roast pork.

The sauerkraut I use for this recipe is packaged in plastic bags and sold in the refrigerated section of the supermarket.

½ cup uncooked rice
1 pound ground beef
1 pound ground pork
½ large onion, finely chopped
1 garlic clove, finely chopped
¼ cup grated Parmesan cheese
2 eggs, beaten
1½ teaspoons salt
¼ teaspoon pepper
½ pound cooked roast pork (butt end)
2 tablespoons butter
large head cabbage
16 ounces sauerkraut, drained
1 quart whole tomatoes, mashed
caraway seeds

1. Cook the rice in lightly salted water, according to package directions. Cool slightly. Mix with next eight ingredients for the filling.

2. Slice the pork butt into ½-inch slices, brown quickly in butter, and set aside.

3. Blanch the cabbage in boiling water, being careful to keep the cabbage leaves whole. To do this, remove the core from the head of cabbage and place the cabbage in enough boiling water to completely cover it. Cook until the leaves become tender. Remove each outside layer as it cooks. Place the cooked cabbage leaves in cold water. Drain.

4. Preheat the oven to 350°F. Fill and roll all cabbage leaves. In a deep roasting pan, layer the sauerkraut, tomatoes, and cabbage rolls. Add the roast pork around the cabbage rolls. Season the tomatoes with caraway seeds. Cover and bake for at least 1 hour. Add water if the tomatoes and sauerkraut become too dry. Serve hot.

Meats

"It is good against all venome and poyson, taken in meats or boyled in wine and drunken. . . ."

—Turner's Herbal

Garlic can enhance the flavor of meat in a variety of ways. As mentioned in the Introduction, you can pierce a pork roast or leg of lamb with wedges of garlic to achieve a subtly different taste. Garlic perks up the marinades that season steaks and chops, and adds just the right accent of flavor when sautéed with veal or beef cubes. Whole cloves of garlic bestow a mild, almost sweet taste to basked chicken.

The flavor and tenderness of meat are influenced by the amount of fat it contains, which varies from one type of animal to another and from one cut to another. The fat in some meats is highly marbled, or dispersed throughout the meat, which keeps it juicy and contributes to the flavor and aroma of the meat while cooking.

Certain meats are aged by being stored at cold temperatures for a number of days before being marketed, which adds to their flavor and tenderness. The beef sold to the restaurant trade, for example, is aged for about two weeks at temperatures slightly above freezing.

The tenderness of meat is also influenced by the animal's age and its activity level, as well as by the cut of meat and the way it is cooked. Those parts of the animal that have experienced the most activity, such as the neck, shoulder, and legs, tend to be less tender than the loin and rib areas. Use appropriate cooking methods to make each cut of meat as tender as possible. Cook tough cuts of meat slowly in liquids for long periods of time. More tender cuts can be roasted, broiled, or pan fried.

Beef is rich in protein, iron, calcium, and B vitamins. Federal inspection is required of all beef that is transported across state lines, but grading of beef for flavor and tenderness is up to the meat packers.

The three grades beginning with the best, are "prime," "choice," and "good." Almost all prime cuts are sold to restaurants. Choice grades are abundantly available for retail consumption.

The best tasting and most tender veal, and thus the most expensive veal, comes from milk-fed calves, 5–12 weeks old. Such veal is pale grayish pink, with little or no marbling of fat. When a calf's diet is primarily grass or grain (rather than milk), its flesh becomes dark pink to reddish in appearance, resulting in a less delicate flavor and a less tender cut.

Lamb, which is rich in iron, niacin, thiamine, and riboflavin, is marketed at 6–8 months. The best cuts of lamb are bright pink with an abundance of marbled white fat.

Pork is sold fresh or processed as ham, bacon, or sausages. When selecting fresh pork, choose meat that has a whitish pink color and is marbled with lots of white fat. The pinker the meat, the older the animal. Pork is a good source of B vitamins and iron. It must be thoroughly cooked to an internal temperature of 170°F. to insure the destruction of any harmful organisms and for maximum flavor. A fresh pork roast is done if the juices run clear when the meat is pierced.

Chicken is the primary poultry featured in these recipes. This popular food has fewer calories, cholesterol, and fat than many other meats. It is an excellent source of high-quality protein, and it contains abundant amounts of calcium and phosphorus. Chickens are available in several varieties including broilers, capons, and stewers. Broilers are marketed at 7–9 weeks and average less than 4 pounds. Because these birds are so young, they are good for frying or broiling when little, if any, water is required. Capons are castrated male chickens which grow plump, with abundant white meat, in about 20 weeks to about 5–7 pounds. Stewers are the most inexpensive of the chicken varieties mentioned. These aged hens, beyond their egg-laying prime, must be slowly cooked in lots of liquid for a long time to become tender. They impart a good flavor to soups.

When selecting chicken, look for the USDA inspection mark as an assurance of wholesomeness. Grading, which is not mandatory by federal law, is an indication of the quality of the chicken. For the best possible chicken, select only USDA-inspected, fresh Grade A chicken, with a clean scent, firm flesh, and bright, even color ranging from yellow to white.

The game recipes presented here include venison, elk, rabbit, and pheasant. Some people are put off by what has been described as the "gaminess" of such meat. This reaction may stem from the experiences of people who have eaten game that was past its prime or not properly prepared. The fat of the elk or venison is what gives it its sometimes strong flavor. Thus, it is best to trim off almost all excess fat before cooking. With venison or elk roasts, slow baking with sherry or white wine seems to reduce the gaminess, as do accents of garlic. With game also, the age of the animal, its diet, and the cut of the meat are crucial factors contributing to its flavor and tenderness.

Pheasant is mild and flavorful, almost indistinguishable in taste from chicken. It tends to be somewhat drier than chicken, however, so be especially careful not to overcook it. Commercially grown pheasants are available (usually frozen) in specialty meat stores. Rabbits also are raised commercially and are available cleaned and frozen in specialty meat shops.

veal roast

SERVES 4–6
PREPARATION TIME:
2½–2¾ HOURS

1 3-pound boneless veal roast
1 teaspoon salt
½–1 teaspoon pepper
1–2 tablespoons parsley, chopped
6–7 garlic cloves, chopped
¼ cup vegetable oil
½ cup water
2 carrots, peeled

1. Preheat the oven to 325°F.

2. Season the veal with salt, pepper, parsley, and garlic.

3. Place the veal in a roasting pan. Add the oil and water, and place the carrots around the meat. Cover the pan with heavy-duty aluminum foil. Bake for 2½ hours, or until a meat thermometer registers 160°–170°F., and the veal juices run clear when the roast is pierced. Serve.

breaded veal cubes

SERVES 4–6
PREPARATION TIME:
60 MINUTES

¾ cup breadcrumbs
2–3 garlic cloves, finely chopped
2 tablespoons fresh parsley,
    chopped
2 tablespoons grated Parmesan
    cheese
½ teaspoon salt
⅛ tablespoon pepper
1–1½ pounds boneless veal cubes
5–6 tablespoons flour
1 egg, beaten with 2–3
    tablespoons water
vegetable oil

Veal cubes, also marketed as boneless stewing veal, are fairly inexpensive cuts of veal. When cooked according to the directions in this recipe, they become quite tender and flavorful.

1. Toss the breadcrumbs with the garlic, parsley, grated cheese, salt, and pepper.

2. Slice each veal cube crosswise into 2 or 3 thin slices. Dust in the flour, dip in the well-beaten egg, and coat with the seasoned breadcrumbs.

3. Brown the veal quickly in a small amount of oil. Then place it on a rack in a frying pan. Add a little water to the pan (do not let the water come above the top of the rack). Simmer, covered, until the veal is tender, about 30 minutes. Add more water as the original amount evaporates. The veal is ready when it can be easily pierced with a fork. Serve.

stuffed breast of veal

SERVES 4–6
PREPARATION TIME:
2 HOURS

1 4–5-pound breast of veal
3–4 slices Italian bread
½ cup milk
2 garlic cloves, chopped
¼ cup chopped onion
1–2 teaspoons raisins, chopped
1 tablespoon vegetable oil
1 tablespoon butter
⅓ cup breakfast cereal (such as cornflakes or a crispy rice cereal), crumbled
2 eggs, beaten
salt and pepper
¾ cup breadcrumbs
2 tablespoons grated Parmesan cheese
2–3 tablespoons fresh parsley, chopped
1½ tablespoons mayonnaise
2–3 tablespoons vegetable oil
1 tablespoon ketchup
1¼ cups water

Check with your grocer to find out when this special cut of veal is available. Ask the butcher to make a large pocket in the veal for the stuffing. You will need 4–6-inch skewers to fasten the pocket once the veal is stuffed.

1. Soak the veal in cold water for 3–4 minutes. Drain for 10 minutes in a colander. Dry with a paper towel.

2. Soak the bread in ¼ cup of the milk. Then squeeze out excess milk, crumble the bread into loose pieces, and set aside.

3. Sauté the garlic, onion, and raisins in oil and butter for 3–5 minutes, until the onion becomes transparent. Cool. Add the moist bread and the remaining ¼ cup milk, the cereal, eggs, salt, pepper, breadcrumbs, cheese, and parsley. If the mixture is too dry, add more milk, a tablespoon at a time.

4. Preheat the oven to 350°F. Stuff the filling into the pocket of the veal and fasten the opening with 4–6 small skewers. Season the veal with salt and pepper and place it in a roasting pan.

5. Combine the mayonnaise, oil, and ketchup. Add ¼ cup water and stir well. Pour the glaze over the veal. Add 1 cup water to the pan.

6. Cover the pan with foil and bake for 1½ hours or longer, until the meat is very tender. As the glaze dries up while baking, add more water to the pan. Turn the veal breast over once, halfway through the suggested cooking time. When it is done, the meat should separate easily from the bone when prodded with a fork. Serve.

veal roulades

SERVES 6–8
PREPARATION TIME:
60–70 MINUTES

8 thin veal cutlets
salt and pepper to taste
8 slices boiled ham
8 slices Swiss cheese
2 tablespoons flour
3 tablespoons butter
1 teaspoon vegetable oil
4 ounces sliced mushrooms
¼ cup chopped onion
2 garlic cloves, chopped
2 tablespoons butter
1 teaspoon flour
1 tablespoon lemon juice
2¼ cups hot water
1 beef bouillon cube
3 tablespoons uncooked rice

1. Season each cutlet with salt and pepper. Place one slice of ham and cheese on each cutlet, roll, and secure with toothpicks or kitchen twine.

2. Dredge the rolled veal in flour to coat lightly. Then brown the veal in butter (3 tablespoons) and oil for 5–7 minutes, turning as needed to brown evenly. Set aside. Preheat the oven to 400°F.

3. In the same pan, sauté the mushrooms, onion, and garlic in 2 tablespoons butter for 3–5 minutes, until the onion is soft. Stir in 1 teaspoon flour and the lemon juice.

4. Place the veal in a casserole dish, add the vegetables, 2¼ cups water, the bouillon cube, and the rice. Cover and bake for 30 minutes, or until a fork easily pierces the meat, basting occasionally. Remove the toothpicks or string. Serve.

veal and lima beans

SERVES 4–6
PREPARATION TIME:
60–70 MINUTES

1½ pounds veal shanks (with
   the bone)
4–6 tablespoons vegetable oil
salt and pepper to taste
1 cup sliced onion
2–3 garlic cloves, chopped
1 teaspoon parsley, chopped
⅛ teaspoon oregano
10–12 ounces lima beans (about
   2½ cups)
8 ounces tomato sauce
2 cups water
¼ teaspoon sugar (optional)

Veal shanks are relatively inexpensive cuts of veal which, when cooked in this stew, become tender and delicious. Be sure to select the meatiest pieces. Use fresh lima beans, if possible, or frozen—but not canned.

1. Sauté the veal in 3–4 tablespoons oil over medium-high heat, stirring frequently, for 7–10 minutes, or until the meat is well browned. Season lightly with salt and pepper.

2. Add the onions, garlic, parsley, and oregano, and continue to sauté. And 1–2 tablespoons vegetable oil, if needed. When the onions become soft, add the lima beans, lightly seasoned with salt. Add ¼ cup water, cover, and simmer for 5–7 minutes.

3. Mix the tomato sauce with the water and sugar and pour over the veal and lima beans. Bring to a low boil, reduce the heat, and simmer in a covered pan for 35–45 minutes, until the veal is tender and can easily be pushed off the bones. Add more water as needed. Serve.

stuffed veal roll

SERVES 6
PREPARATION TIME:
2½ HOURS

Mortadella is an Italian cold cut available in Italian grocery shops or delicatessens.
   The breast of veal must be removed from the bones in one piece. You might want to ask your butcher to do this for you. If so, ask him to give you the bones.
   You will need kitchen twine to tie the veal roll once it's stuffed.

1 4–5-pound breast of veal
salt and pepper to taste
2 tablespoons fresh parsley,
   chopped
2 tablespoons grated Parmesan
   cheese
6 slices mortadella
6 slices boiled ham
3–4 tablespoons vegetable oil
2 carrots, peeled and sliced
2 stalks celery, chopped
1 large onion, chopped
2 garlic cloves, chopped
3 chicken bouillon cubes

1. Remove the veal from the bones in one piece and reserve the bones. Trim off excess fat. Spread out the veal and season it lightly with salt and pepper. Sprinkle the parsley and grated cheese over the meat. Layer it with the cold cuts. Starting at the wide end of the veal, roll it tightly and secure it with kitchen twine. Tie the cord at 1-inch intervals across the rolled veal.

2. Heat the vegetable oil in a dutch oven. Brown the veal and the bones over medium-high to high heat for 10–15 minutes. Add the chopped vegetables and garlic and sauté for 5–8 minutes. Season the vegetables with salt and pepper.

3. Dissolve the bouillon cubes in 1 cup boiling water. Add to the dutch oven.

4. Bring the broth to a boil, reduce the heat, and cook the veal (covered) on low for 1½ hours, or until tender. Turn occasionally. Remove the bones and the cord. Serve slices of veal topped with veal stock.

moussaka

SERVES 8
PREPARATION TIME:
1½ HOURS

2 large eggplants
vegetable oil
¾ cup chopped onions
2 garlic cloves, finely chopped
1 tablespoon fresh parsley,
  chopped
3–4 tablespoons vegetable oil
1 pound ground lamb
1 teaspoon salt
¼ teaspoon pepper
dash cinnamon
½ cup tomato sauce
½ cup cornflake crumbs
½ cup grated Parmesan cheese
2 tablespoons butter
2 tablespoons flour
1 cup milk
½ cup ricotta cheese
1 egg, beaten
dash nutmeg

For the best ground lamb, do not rely on packaged pre-ground lamb. It's better to select an attractive cut, such as a portion of the shoulder, and ask your butcher to trim the fat and grind the meat.

1. Preheat the oven to 425°F. Peel the eggplants, and cut them into ¼-inch-thick slices.

2. Cover the surface of a cookie sheet with a thin film of vegetable oil and put the cookie sheet in the oven for a minute or two, to heat the oil. Then add the eggplant slices to the cookie sheet and bake for 7–10 minutes, until soft. Add more oil as needed. Remove from the oven and drain in a colander and then on paper towels. Reduce the oven temperature to 350°F.

3. Meanwhile, sauté the onions, garlic and parsley in 3–4 tablespoons vegetable oil for 3–5 minutes, until the onions are tender. Add the lamb. Season with salt, pepper, and cinnamon. When browned, add the tomato sauce and, if too dry, some water; simmer for 5 minutes. Remove from the heat.

4. Layer the eggplant and the ground lamb mixture alternately in a medium-size casserole dish, finishing off with an eggplant layer on top. Top the casserole with cornflake crumbs and grated cheese.

5. Melt the butter in a saucepan. When it begins to bubble, add the flour, all at once, and stir quickly to avoid lumps. Add the milk, a little at a time, to keep the mixture smooth. Allow it to reach a slow

boil and to thicken somewhat. Remove from the heat and cool slightly. Then add the ricotta and egg. Season with nutmeg. Pour over the eggplant. Bake at 350°F. for 30–40 minutes. Cover loosely with foil if the top gets too brown.

<u>roast leg of lamb</u>

SERVES 6–8
PREPARATION TIME:
2 HOURS

leg of lamb (6–8 pounds)
5–6 garlic cloves, cut in half
3–4 tablespoons fresh parsley, chopped
1 tablespoon fresh rosemary leaves (optional)
salt and pepper to taste

Select fresh young lamb, light in color, with a generous marbling of white fat and bones that are moist and porous.

1. Preheat the oven to 325°F.

2. Using a sharp paring knife, trim any excess fat from the lamb. Then make about 10 ½-inch slits in the surface of the lamb and fill each with garlic and parsley. Sprinkle the rosemary over the lamb. Season lightly with salt and heavily with pepper.

3. Bake the lamb, without water, in an uncovered roasting pan for 2 or more hours, until so tender that a fork easily pierces the lamb and a meat thermometer reaches 150°–160°F. (for medium). Serve.

rolled stuffed steaks

SERVES 4
PREPARATION TIME:
1½ HOURS

Ask your butcher for thin-sliced round steaks and figure on one steak per serving. After the steaks have been filled, rolled, and browned, they can be served either in tomato sauce or in brown gravy. If you plan to use tomato sauce, prepare it ahead of time according to the recipe on page 82 and freeze it until needed. These can be frozen after they are stuffed and rolled, but before they are browned.

You will need some string or kitchen twine on hand to tie the steaks.

4 slices round steak (1½–2 pounds total)
salt and pepper to taste
3–4 tablespoons vegetable oil

Filling:

2 large eggs, well beaten
½ heaping teaspoon salt
½ teaspoon pepper
2 garlic cloves, finely chopped
4 tablespoons fresh parsley, finely chopped
⅓ cup grated Parmesan cheese
½ cup breadcrumbs
1–3 tablespoons milk
1 quart tomato sauce (from the recipe on page 82)

1. Combine the eggs, salt, pepper, garlic, and parsley. Add the grated cheese, breadcrumbs, and milk. The mixture will be thick and moist.

2. Lightly season each piece of steak with salt and pepper. Spread the filling evenly over each slice of steak to within ⅜ inch of the edges. Roll the steak firmly, but not too tightly. Tie each rolled steak with string: First, wrap the string lengthwise around each rolled steak, then cross the string as if you were wrapping a package, and bring it back and forth over the rolled steak at 1-inch intervals. Tie securely.

3. Heat the vegetable oil in a stockpot, and brown the rolled steaks in the hot oil. Then cover them completely with tomato sauce, and cook over low heat for 60 or more minutes, until the meat is tender when pierced with a fork. Remove the string and serve at once.

If you prefer, these rolled steaks can be served with brown gravy instead of tomato sauce.

Brown Gravy:

3–4 tablespoons vegetable oil
¼ cup chopped onion
4 tablespoons fresh parsley, chopped
2 large garlic cloves, finely chopped
4 ounces mushrooms, chopped
4 cups water
4–5 beef bouillon cubes
1½ teaspoons browning and seasoning sauce (e.g., Gravy Master)
3 tablespoons butter or margarine
4 tablespoons flour
salt and pepper to taste

1. Heat the vegetable oil in a skillet and brown the rolled steaks in the hot oil. Remove them from the pan. In the same pan, sauté the onion, parsley and garlic for 3–5 minutes. Add the mushrooms and saute for 1–2 minutes longer.

2. Heat 4 cups water in a saucepan. Add the beef bouillon cubes and allow them to dissolve. Add the browning and seasoning sauce and the butter. Bring to a simmer. Preheat the oven to 350°F.

3. Meanwhile, combine the flour with enough cold water (3–4 tablespoons) to make a smooth paste. Add several tablespoons of bouillon broth to the flour mixture. Beat until smooth. Then add the flour mixture very slowly to the simmering bouillon broth, stirring rapidly to keep the flour from forming lumps. Simmer for 5–7 minutes more.

4. Place the browned rolled steaks and the onion, garlic, and mushrooms in a roasting pan. Pour in the gravy to completely cover them. Add more water if necessary. Cover and bake for 45 minutes, or until tender. Remove the string and serve.

pot roast

SERVES 4–6
PREPARATION TIME:
2½ HOURS

1 large onion, sliced (about 1 cup)
2 garlic cloves, chopped
¼–⅓ cup vegetable oil
1 2¾–3-pound chuck roast
3 tablespoons fresh parsley,
    chopped
¼ teaspoon pepper
2 carrots, peeled and cut into
    large pieces
¼ cup white wine
½ cup water
salt to taste

1. Preheat the oven to 325°F.

2. Sauté the onion and garlic in 2–3 tablespoons of the vegetable oil.

3. Place the meat in a roasting pan. Pour 2–3 tablespoons vegetable oil over the meat. Season with the parsley and pepper. Top with the sauteéd onion and garlic. Add the carrots, wine, and water. Cover and bake in the oven for 2 hours or longer, until tender. Season with salt about 10 minutes before removing from the oven. Serve.

beef stew

SERVES 6
PREPARATION TIME:
1½ HOURS

2 pounds chuck steaks
2 tablespoons vegetable oil
1 garlic clove, chopped
1 medium-size onion, chopped
4 ounces mushrooms, sliced
4 large carrots, peeled and sliced
    ¼ inch thick
4 stalks celery, sliced ½-inch
    thick
celery leaves
1 teaspoon parsley, chopped
½ teaspoon oregano
1 teaspoon salt
½ teaspoon pepper
1½ cups water
2 beef bouillon cubes
8 ounces tomato sauce
6 medium-size potatoes, peeled
    and cubed into 1-inch sizes
16 ounces frozen peas (or 2 cups
    fresh)

Chuck steak is a fairly inexpensive, yet tasty cut of meat, which cooks up quite tender in this stew.

1. Remove the excess fat and bones from the chuck steaks and cut them into 1-inch cubes. In a 3-inch-deep frying pan, sauté the meat in oil over medium-high heat until browned on all sides (10–15 minutes).

2. Add the garlic, onion, and mushrooms and sauté for another 5 minutes, stirring periodically.

3. Add the carrots, celery, parsley, and oregano. Season with salt and pepper. Cook over medium-high heat for 10–15 minutes, stirring occasionally. Add about 1½ cups water and the bouillon cubes. After the bouillon cubes dissolve, add the tomato sauce and the potatoes and cook (covered) for about 25 minutes, until the potatoes and meat are tender. Stir often. Continue to add more water as needed to keep the stew juicy. Add the peas during the last 15 minutes of cooking time. Serve hot.

korean beef and vegetables

SERVES 4
PREPARATION TIME:
60 MINUTES

For a more authentic version of this recipe, Korean vermicelli, made from potato starch, may be substituted. These fine, almost transparent noodles are available in Oriental grocery stores. Cook according to package directions.

Put the steak in the freezer for 30–60 minutes ahead of time. Partial freezing will make it easier to slice.

10 ounces fresh broccoli spears
2 large carrots, peeled
4 ounces mushrooms, sliced
4 tablespoons butter
5 green onions (1 bunch)
1 garlic clove, finely chopped
½ pound sirloin steak
   (partially frozen)
1–2 tablespoons sesame oil
salt and pepper to taste
¼ cup water
¼ cup soy sauce
4–5 ounces thin spaghetti, broken
   in half

1. Chop the broccoli into 2-inch pieces and cut the carrots into 2-inch julienne strips. Blanch the broccoli and carrots in boiling, lightly salted water for about 5 minutes. Do not overcook. The vegetables should be tender but crisp. Drain.

2. Sauté the mushrooms in 1 tablespoon butter for 1–2 minutes. Set aside.

3. Cut the onions into 2-inch pieces. Sauté with the chopped garlic in 1 tablespoon butter for 1–2 minutes. Set aside.

4. Slice the steak into ⅛-inch-thick strips and cook in 2 tablespoons butter and 1–2 tablespoons sesame oil over medium-high heat, just until the meat loses its red color. Add the broccoli, carrots, mushrooms, and onions. Season with salt and pepper.

5. Meanwhile, cook the spaghetti in boiling, lightly salted water for about 7 minutes, until tender but not overcooked. Drain. Combine the spaghetti with the steak and vegetables. Add the water and soy sauce. Stir, cover, and simmer for 5 minutes. Serve.

szechuan-style beef and green peppers

SERVES 4
PREPARATION TIME:
60 MINUTES

Sirloin steaks are derived from the cut of beef between the short loin and rump sections. These steaks are named after the type of bone each cut contains, such as pin-bone sirloin, flat-bone sirloin, and wedge-bone sirloin. Select steaks with ample marbling of fat. Before slicing your steak, place it in the freezer for 30–60 minutes. It will slice more easily when it is partially frozen. Try this dish served over white or brown rice.

1 small onion, sliced (about ½ cup)
2 garlic cloves, finely chopped
3–4 green bell peppers, sliced
3 tablespoons sesame oil
1 tablespoon butter
1 pound sirloin steak or top round steak, thinly sliced
salt and pepper to taste
1 tablespoon cornstarch
1 tablespoon water

1. Sauté the onion, garlic, and peppers in oil and butter until the peppers are tender but slightly crisp. Remove the vegetables from the pan and reserve the oil.

2. Cook the sliced steak in the reserved hot oil just until the meat loses its red color. Season with salt and pepper.

3. Return the vegetables to the frying pan. Dissolve the cornstarch in 1 tablespoon water and pour over the steak and vegetables. Heat thoroughly, allowing the flavors of all the ingredients to blend. Serve over rice, if desired.

cantonese beef with snow peas

SERVES 4
PREPARATION TIME:
30–45 MINUTES PLUS 9
HOURS TO MARINATE

1 cup cooking sherry
¼ cup soy sauce
1 garlic clove, crushed
¼ teaspoon ground ginger
1 pound flank steak
1 egg white
1½ teaspoons soy sauce
1½ teaspoons water
1 tablespoon cornstarch
2 garlic cloves, finely chopped
¾–1 cup vegetable oil
½ pound snow peas
¾ teaspoon salt
½ teaspoon sugar
1 tablespoon cooking sherry
½ teaspoon cornstarch dissolved
   in 2 tablespoons water
1 8-ounce can sliced water
   chestnuts (optional)

Select crisp-looking snow peas with no sign of yellow. They are stir-fried very briefly, so that they retain their crunchiness.
This dish can be served over white or brown rice.

1. Combine the 1 cup cooking sherry, soy sauce, crushed garlic, and ground ginger to make a marinade. Marinate the flank steak in the refrigerator for about 9 hours to tenderize and flavor the meat.

2. Slice the meat very thin (⅛-inch thick). The cuts should be angled across the grain of the meat for maximum tenderness.

3. Combine the egg white, soy sauce, water, and 1 tablespoon cornstarch. Add the chopped garlic and sliced beef and stir until the beef is coated with the egg white mixture.

4. Stir-fry the beef in hot oil (about 400°F.) in a skillet or wok for 1–2 minutes, just until the beef loses its red color. Remove the beef with a slotted spoon.

5. Discard all but about 3 tablespoons of the oil. Reheat the oil to 375°–400°F. Add the snow peas. Season with salt, sugar, and sherry and·stir-fry for 1–2 minutes, until tender but crisp. Add the beef and cook for 1 minute. Add the dissolved cornstarch and toss briefly until the sauce is thickened. Add the water chestnuts, heat through, and serve immediately.

tomato marinated steak

SERVES 4
PREPARATION TIME:
30–40 MINUTES PLUS OVER-
NIGHT TO MARINATE

1½ cups tomato juice (or
   multi-vegetable juice)
½ cup lemon juice
⅓ cup soy sauce
¼ cup vegetable oil
3 large garlic cloves, chopped
½ teaspoon pepper
⅛ teaspoon ground ginger
1 tablespoon sugar
1½–2 pounds london broil or
   flank steak
1–2 tablespoons cornstarch

To marinate the meat for this recipe, place the meat and the marinade in a self-sealing plastic bag large enough for the meat to lie flat. Using a plastic bag for marinating makes turning the meat easy and makes clean-up a snap.

1. Make a marinade by combining all the ingredients except the meat and the cornstarch. Pierce the meat in several places with a sharp knife, cover it with the marinade, and refrigerate it overnight, turning occasionally.

2. Preheat the broiler. Remove the meat and reserve the marinade. Broil the steak for 8–10 minutes on each side, or until cooked to your preference.

3. Meanwhile, in a small saucepan, mix a small amount of the marinade with the cornstarch until smooth. Gradually add the remaining marinade and cook over low heat, stirring until thickened. Makes approximately 3 cups sauce. Cut the steak into thin slices, on an angle. Pour the sauce over the steak and serve hot.

meat loaf

SERVES 6
PREPARATION TIME:
75–90 MINUTES

½ cup chopped onion
1 garlic clove, chopped
1 tablespoon butter
2 tablespoons vegetable oil
4 ounces mushrooms, chopped
4 slices day-old Italian bread
½–1 cup milk
1½ pounds ground veal, beef,
   and pork
1½ teaspoons salt
¼ teaspoon pepper
2 tablespoons fresh parsley,
   chopped
2 eggs, beaten
breadcrumbs (optional)

Turn an ordinary meat loaf into a more flavorful one by adding ground veal and ground pork to the usual ground beef. Use your hands to mix the ingredients to ensure even distribution of all the flavors.

1. Sauté the onion and garlic in butter and oil for about 3 minutes, until the onion is transparent and soft. Remove the onion and garlic and set aside. Sauté the mushrooms in the remaining butter and oil for 3–5 minutes, drain, and set aside.

2. Soak the bread in milk until soft. Crumble the bread into small pieces; squeeze out excess milk. When moistened and crumbled into pieces, the bread should equal about 1 heaping cup.

3. Preheat the oven to 400°F. Combine all the ingredients, adding some breadcrumbs if the mixture is too soft. Form the mixture into an oblong shape and place in a greased pan.

4. Bake in the oven for 45–60 minutes, uncovered. Serve.

rosemary and garlic chicken

SERVES 4
PREPARATION TIME:
1½ HOURS

1 whole 3–4 pound chicken, cut
   into parts
4–5 tablespoons butter
4–5 tablespoons margarine
1–2 tablespoons vegetable oil
2 garlic cloves finely chopped
2 bay leaves
1 teaspoon rosemary leaves,
   crushed

Batter:

2 eggs, beaten
5–6 tablespoons flour
¼ teaspoon salt
⅛ teaspoon pepper
1 garlic clove, finely chopped
1–2 tablespoons water

Chicken is most economical when purchased whole and then cut into parts, a procedure which is easily mastered after a few attempts. Using a very sharp knife or poultry shears, halve the chicken by cutting along the breastbone and then down along one side of the backbone. Locate the joints for the hips, wings, and thighs and sever at these points. Cut the remaining pieces into single serving sizes.

1. Rinse the chicken in cold water. Drain. Pat dry with paper towels. Trim off and discard excess fat.

2. Combine all the ingredients for the batter. The batter should be slightly thick. If too thick, add a little more water. Dip the chicken pieces in the batter.

3. In a large frying pan, heat the butter, margarine, and oil to sizzling hot and add the chicken. Fry, uncovered, over medium-high to high heat, allowing the shortening to bubble around the chicken for about 15 minutes, until the chicken is golden brown and crisp. Meanwhile, preheat the oven to 350°F.

4. Remove the chicken from the pan and place it in a baking dish. Discard any excess oil, then sauté the garlic, bay leaves, and rosemary in the 1–2 tablespoons remaining shortening for 30–60 seconds. Pour over the chicken. Cover the baking dish with foil and bake for 15 minutes. Then remove the foil and bake for 15 more minutes, or until done. Baste and turn the chicken as necessary. Serve hot.

lemon and herb chicken

SERVES 4
PREPARATION TIME:
60–75 MINUTES

Select a young broiler-fryer chicken for this recipe. Look for firm flesh and even-colored skin. Choose a fresh, not frozen, chicken and use it within two days of purchase. Fresh chickens tend to be more juicy than frozen ones, and self-basting juices are important when broiling.

1 3½-pound chicken
½ cup vegetable oil
2 tablespoons lemon juice
3 bay leaves, crumbled
1 tablespoon tarragon
1½ teaspoons pepper
1 tablespoon seasoned salt
1 garlic clove, chopped finely
1½ teaspoons thyme
1 tablespoon fresh basil, chopped
1 lemon, thinly sliced

1. Preheat the broiler.
2. Split the chicken in half. Rinse in cold water and pat dry with paper towels.
3. Combine the vegetable oil and all the seasonings. Allow the seasonings to flavor the oil for about 10 minutes.
4. Place the chicken halves in a greased baking pan, skin-side down. Rub the oil and seasonings over the chicken. Broil for 10–15 minutes on each side. Watch the chicken carefully as it broils, moving it farther from the broiler if necessary to avoid burning. Baste often.
5. When the chicken is browned, turn off the broiler and bake at 350°F. for 15–25 minutes, or until tender. Place the lemon slices over the chicken during the last 10 minutes of baking time. Serve at once.

sherry-glazed chicken

SERVES 4
PREPARATION TIME:
60 MINUTES

1 3-pound chicken
⅓ cup vegetable oil
2 garlic cloves, chopped finely
1¼ teaspoons oregano
1 teaspoon salt
¼ teaspoon pepper
½ cup cooking sherry

1. Rinse the chicken in cold water. Pat dry. Cut into parts and trim off the excess fat.

2. Heat the oil in a dutch oven. Add the chicken. Season with garlic, oregano, salt, and pepper. Cook with the lid ajar over medium-high heat for 10–15 minutes, until browned.

3. Cover the pot, reduce the heat to medium-low, and cook for 25–30 more minutes, or until done, turning occasionally.

4. Transfer the chicken to a serving dish. Discard all but ¼–⅓ cup of the oil in the pot. Add the sherry to the remaining oil, and allow this mixture to simmer for 5 minutes. Scrape free any chicken sticking to the bottom of the pan and stir it into the glaze. Spoon the glaze over the chicken and serve.

garlicky roast chicken

SERVES 4
PREPARATION TIME:
60–70 MINUTES

1 5-pound roasting chicken
4 tablespoons butter
1 teaspoon crushed rosemary
  leaves
1 teaspoon ground sage
1½ teaspoons ground thyme
salt and pepper to taste
20 whole garlic cloves, peeled
3 tablespoons lemon juice
½ cup water

Select a medium-size roasting chicken with firm flesh and good color. Roasters are generally several weeks older than broilers and slightly larger, with tender meat. An abundance of garlic cloves is used to flavor this chicken, but, due to the lengthy cooking process, the taste of the garlic is sweet.

1. Preheat the oven to 375°F.

2. Rinse the chicken in cold water. Drain and pat dry.

3. Soften the butter and season it with the rosemary, sage, and thyme. Place the chicken in a roasting pan and rub it with the seasoned butter. Sprinkle with salt and pepper. Place the 20 garlic cloves in and around the chicken. Add the lemon juice to the chicken cavity. Add ½ cup water to the pan.

4. Cover the pan tightly with aluminum foil. Bake for 45 minutes, or until the chicken is tender. Raise the oven temperature to 425°F., remove the foil, and cook for 15 more minutes to brown the skin. Then serve.

coconut chicken for two

SERVES 2
PREPARATION TIME:
45–60 MINUTES

1 pound boneless chicken breasts,
   skinned and cubed
1 garlic clove, finely chopped
5 tablespoons butter
¾ teaspoon ground ginger
½ teaspoon salt
⅓ cup toasted coconut
1 cup heavy cream
2 bananas, quartered
1 cup sliced peaches

Chicken breasts can dry out if they are overcooked so be careful to sauté them for only a couple of minutes. This entrée can be served over 4–6 ounces angel hair pasta, cooked according to package directions.

1. Sauté the chicken pieces and garlic in 4 tablespoons of the butter for 2–3 minutes, just until the chicken loses its pink color. Season with the ginger and salt. Add half of the toasted coconut to coat the chicken. Pour in the cream, cover, and cook over medium heat for 5–10 minutes, or until the chicken is tender.

2. In a separate pan, sauté the bananas in 1 tablespoon butter for 1–2 minutes. Add the peaches and cook for 1–2 minutes longer.

3. Remove the chicken and arrange it on a platter. Spoon the sauce over the chicken and arrange the fruit on top. Sprinkle the remaining coconut over all. Serve immediately.

chicken l'orange salad

SERVES 4–6
PREPARATION TIME:
30 MINUTES PLUS 3 HOURS
TO POACH, COOL, AND
CHILL

1 3½-pound whole chicken
1 teaspoon salt
1 carrot, peeled
2 stalks celery
1 small onion
1 garlic clove
½ cup chopped celery
2 hard-boiled eggs, sliced
1 cup mandarin orange sections
½ cup sour cream
½ cup mayonnaise
1 tablespoon heavy cream
1 tablespoon vinegar
1 tablespoon vegetable oil
½ teaspoon dill
salt and pepper to taste
1 garlic clove, finely chopped
lettuce leaves
10–12 black olives, pitted
¼ cup sliced almonds

Save the liquid that you use for poaching the chicken—it can serve as the basis for a soup stock or for use in a cream sauce or other chicken-flavored sauce. Chill the broth, skim the fat off the top, and then freeze it for use within 1½–2 months.

1. Several hours ahead of time, place the chicken, breast-side down, in a dutch oven. Pour in enough water to half cover the chicken. Add the salt, carrot, celery, onion, and garlic. Cover and bring to a hard boil. Reduce to a simmer and cook for 45–50 minutes, or until tender when pierced with a fork. Cool in the broth. When the chicken has cooled, remove the meat from the bones and cut it into small chunks. Discard the skin and bones. Reserve the broth for soup stock.

2. In a large bowl, combine the chicken with the celery, sliced eggs, and mandarin oranges. Mix all the remaining ingredients, except the lettuce, olives, and almonds, and pour ¾–1 cup of the dressing over the chicken. Toss gently. Arrange a bed of lettuce leaves on a serving dish and spoon the salad onto the lettuce. Garnish with black olives and sliced almonds. Chill for 1 hour before serving.

artichoke chicken casserole

SERVES 4
PREPARATION TIME:
75 MINUTES

Artichoke hearts, which are easy to find either frozen or canned, are rich in calcium and potassium. The rice in this dish is used only to absorb some of the juices—it's not sufficient to serve four people.

1 whole chicken, cut into parts
6 tablespoons flour
⅛ teaspoon salt
⅛ teaspoon pepper
¼ cup vegetable oil
1 tablespoon butter
10–12 whole mushrooms
6–8 artichoke hearts
2 green peppers, sliced
1 small onion, sliced
2 garlic cloves, chopped
3 tablespoons fresh parsley,
  chopped
4–5 tablespoons vegetable oil
4–5 ripe plum tomatoes, peeled
  (2–3 cups)
1 teaspoon oregano
salt and pepper to taste
¼ teaspoon sugar (to taste)
3 tablespoons uncooked rice
½ cup white wine

1. Dredge the chicken parts in flour seasoned with the salt and pepper. Fry in ¼ cup hot oil and butter for 15 minutes, or until golden brown. Drain on paper towels. Place in a casserole dish. Preheat the oven to 350°F.

2. Sauté the mushrooms and artichoke hearts in the same oil for 3–4 minutes. Add to the casserole dish.

3. Sauté the peppers, onion, garlic, and parsley in 4–5 tablespoons vegetable oil for 10 minutes, or until the onion is soft. Add the tomatoes and season with oregano, salt, pepper, and sugar. Pour this mixture over the chicken.

4. Add the rice and the wine to the casserole dish. Cover and bake for 40 minutes, or until the chicken is tender. Serve at once.

mandarin chicken for two

SERVES 2
PREPARATION TIME:
30–60 MINUTES

Mandarin oranges are characterized by their sweet flavor, few seeds, segments that easily separate, and skins that easily peel. The name is derived from their original cultivation in China. They are now grown abundantly in Japan and California and are available fresh or canned and packed in water.

1 teaspoon cornstarch
1½ tablespoons soy sauce
1 tablespoon cooking sherry
⅛ teaspoon ground ginger
½ teaspoon sugar
1 medium-size green pepper,
   sliced
3 scallions, sliced diagonally
1 tablespoon sesame oil
¾ cup pecan halves
10–12 ounces boneless chicken
   breasts, skinned
1 garlic clove, finely chopped
3 tablespoons butter
1 teaspoon sesame oil
salt and pepper to taste
1 cup mandarin orange sections

1. Dissolve the cornstarch in the soy sauce. Add the sherry, ginger, and sugar. Set aside.

2. Sauté the green pepper and scallions in 1 tablespoon sesame oil for 3–5 minutes. Remove from the pan.

3. Stir-fry the pecans for 1–2 minutes. Remove from the pan.

4. Sauté the chicken with the garlic in butter and 1 teaspoon sesame oil, just until the chicken loses its pink color. Season lightly with salt and pepper. Add the soy sauce mixture and stir until slightly thickened.

5. Return the scallions, green pepper, and pecans to the pan. Add the mandarin oranges. Cover and stir for 1 minute. Serve immediately.

oriental chicken wings

SERVES 2–4
PREPARATION TIME:
1–1½ HOURS

Chicken wings tend to be quite bony—select the meatiest ones you can find for this recipe.

12 chicken wings
1 egg, well beaten
⅔ cup cornstarch
¾ cup vegetable oil
¼–½ teaspoon salt
⅛ teaspoon pepper
⅓ cup chicken stock (or ⅓ bouillon
  cube dissolved in ⅓ cup water)
⅓ cup sugar
⅓ cup white wine vinegar
2 tablespoons ketchup
1 tablespoon soy sauce
2 garlic cloves, finely chopped

1. Separate the chicken wings into three sections by cutting at both joints. Reserve the wing tips for chicken stock or discard them. Dip the remaining pieces in the beaten egg. Roll each piece in cornstarch.

2. Fry the wings in hot vegetable oil over high heat (400°F.) for about 10 minutes, until golden brown. Place in a baking dish and season with salt and pepper.

3. Preheat the oven to 350°F. Combine the remaining ingredients. Pour over the chicken. Bake uncovered for 30 minutes. Serve at once.

chicken wings
in tomato sauce

SERVES 4
PREPARATION TIME:
1½ HOURS

16 chicken wings
4–5 tablespoons vegetable oil
1 cup sliced onions
2 garlic cloves, finely chopped
1 tablespoon parsley, chopped
3 tablespoons vegetable oil
29 ounces tomato purée
1½ cups water
3 tablespoons sugar, to taste
½ teaspoon oregano
salt and pepper to taste
4 medium-size potatoes, peeled
   and quartered
10 ounces fresh or frozen peas

Because chicken wings prepared in this style are "finger-licking good," this dish is a little too messy to serve to guests. It's better to save it for informal, family-only dinners.

1. Preheat the oven to 450°F.

2. Rinse the chicken wings in cold water. Drain. Pat dry with paper towels.

3. Brown the wings in 4–5 tablespoons vegetable oil in a hot oven for about 20 minutes. Drain off excess oil.

4. In a large stockpot, sauté the onions, garlic, and parsley in 3 tablespoons vegetable oil.

5. Add the tomato purée and about 1½ cups water. Season with sugar, oregano, and salt and pepper. Cook over medium-high heat for 5–10 minutes. Add the chicken wings to the tomato purée. Add more water if needed to cover the wings. Add the potatoes, cover, and cook until the potatoes are tender, 30–40 minutes. Add the peas during the last 15 minutes of cooking time. Serve hot.

chicken cacciatora

SERVES 4
PREPARATION TIME:
80 MINUTES

1 whole chicken, cut into parts
3–4 tablespoons vegetable oil
½ cup chopped onion
2 garlic cloves, finely chopped
2 tablespoons fresh parsley,
   chopped
2–3 green peppers, sliced
4 ounces mushrooms, sliced
salt and pepper to taste
¼ cup white wine
16 ounces tomato sauce
2 white potatoes, peeled and cut
   into wedges
1 bay leaf

1. Rinse the chicken parts in cold water. Drain. Pat dry with paper towels. Trim off excess fat.

2. In a large skillet, brown the chicken in vegetable oil over medium-high heat for at least 10 minutes on each side. Add the onion, garlic, parsley, peppers, and mushrooms. Saute 5–10 minutes. Season with salt and pepper. Add the wine and simmer for 2 minutes. Add the tomato sauce, potatoes, bay leaf, and enough water to completely cover the chicken and other ingredients. Cover the skillet and simmer for 30 minutes, or until the potatoes are soft and the meat is tender. Stir occasionally. Serve hot.

apricot-braised pork shoulder

SERVES 6–8
PREPARATION TIME:
2 HOURS

1 3-pound boneless pork shoulder
  roast
1 tablespoon vegetable oil
1½ cups chopped onion
½ cup chopped carrot
1 garlic clove, finely chopped
24 ounces apricot nectar
1 teaspoon dry mustard
1 teaspoon salt

Select a boneless shoulder roast with a firm texture, whitish pink with some marbling of white fat. A boneless, top-loin roast may be substituted.

1. Preheat the oven to 375°F.

2. In a dutch oven, brown the pork shoulder in hot oil. Add the onion, carrot, and garlic and sauté for 3–5 minutes, until the vegetables are tender.

3. Add the apricot nectar, mustard, salt, and enough water to almost cover the pork. Bring to a boil, then cover and bake 1½ hours, until a meat thermometer registers 170°F.

4. Remove the pork from the dutch oven. Boil down the juices until thickened and serve over the pork slices.

sausage and peppers napolitano

SERVES 4
PREPARATION TIME:
60 MINUTES

1¼ pound Italian sausage
  (sectioned)
2 garlic cloves, finely chopped
2 green bell peppers, sliced
1 red bell pepper, sliced
1 medium-size onion, sliced
2–3 tablespoons vegetable oil
1 tablespoon olive oil
salt and pepper to taste
2 tablespoons fresh parsley,
  chopped

Italian sausage is available in several varieties—sweet Italian sausage, fennel sausage, sage-flavored sausage, and hot Italian sausage. Experiment with these until you find the variety you like best.

1. To a large frying pan, add the sausage and ¼–½ inch water. Bring the water to a boil and allow it to evaporate while cooking and turning the sausage. Pierce each piece of sausage in a couple of spots so that the fat will ooze out to baste the sausage, once the water has evaporated. If enough fat does not appear, add more water and allow it to boil and re-evaporate. Cook the sausage, over low to medium heat for 15–20 minutes, until browned.

2. Meanwhile, in a separate pan, covered, fry the peppers, onion, and garlic in both oils for 10–15 minutes, until tender. Season with salt and pepper.

3. Combine the peppers, onion, and sausage in one pan. Drain off any excess fat. Season with the parsley. Sauté for 2–3 minutes. Serve hot.

roast pork and oven-browned potatoes

SERVES 4–6
PREPARATION TIME:
2 HOURS PLUS 12–24 HOURS
TO MARINATE

1 4–5 pound pork loin roast (with
  the bone)
2 large garlic cloves, sliced
¼ teaspoon paprika
¼ teaspoon pepper
⅛ teaspoon ground thyme
2–3 tablespoons vegetable oil
4–6 white potatoes, unpeeled
salt to taste

The center-cut pork loin roast is one of the best cuts of pork for roasting—it is tender, meaty, and flavorful. Select pork with whitish pink flesh marbled with white fat.

1. Using a sharp knife, make several ½-inch-deep slits in the top and sides of the pork roast and stuff with the garlic slices. Mix the remaining spices with the vegetable oil and rub over the roast. Cover with plastic wrap and refrigerate for 12–24 hours.

2. The next day preheat the oven to 325°F. and bake the roast uncovered for 2 hours, or until a meat thermometer reads 165°–170° F.

3. While the roast is cooking, boil the potatoes for 20 minutes, or until tender. Drain, slice lengthwise into halves and add to the roasting pan 20–30 minutes before the roast is done. Baste with the meat juices and turn occasionally until crisp and golden. Serve with the roast.

pork chops and peaches

SERVES 4
PREPARATION TIME:
45–60 MINUTES

3 tablespoons flour
½ teaspoon salt
¼ teaspoon pepper
4 large pork chops
3 tablespoons butter
1 tablespoon vegetable oil
1 garlic clove, chopped
¼ teaspoon ground cloves
⅛ teaspoon nutmeg
¼ teaspoon ground ginger
2 tablespoons butter
4 tablespoons peach preserves
1 cup sliced peaches, canned and
   drained

Select center-cut loin chops, which are among the tastiest cuts of pork. Look for pale, whitish pink flesh and bright white fat. Pork is a good source of iron, niacin, riboflavin, and thiamine. Buttered noodles and broccoli go well with this entrée.

1. Preheat the oven to 350°F.

2. Combine the flour with the salt and pepper and coat the chops. In a large skillet, heat the 3 tablespoons butter and 1 tablespoon oil and sauté the chopped garlic. Do not allow the garlic to darken. Brown the chops briefly in the garlicky oil. Remove the chops from the pan and season with the cloves, nutmeg, and ginger. Reserve the pan drippings.

3. Add the pan drippings and 2 tablespoons butter to a baking dish. Then add the chops. Bake for about 20 minutes. Cover the dish with foil for the first 10 minutes. Turn the chops once. Top with the preserves and peach slices during the last 5 minutes of baking time. Do not overcook. Serve hot.

country-style rabbit

SERVES 4
PREPARATION TIME:
1¾–2 HOURS

1 rabbit, dressed (2–2¼ pounds)
3–4 slices uncooked bacon
vegetable oil
1 teaspoon honey
salt and pepper to taste

Filling:

2 garlic cloves, chopped
½ teaspoon fresh parsley,
    chopped
1 tablespoon grated Parmesan
    cheese
1 tablespoon raisins, finely
    chopped
1 tablespoon chopped onions
3 tablespoons breadcrumbs
1 tablespoon milk
1 egg yolk

The flavor of rabbit is light and delicate, and the meat is low in fat and cholesterol. Wild rabbit may be used, but it tends to be less tender and not as meaty.

1. Preheat the oven to 400°F.

2. Rinse the rabbit in lukewarm, salted water. Drain and pat dry. Cut into parts.

3. Combine all the ingredients for the filling. Using a sharp knife, make pockets in the legs of the rabbit and stuff with the filling. If the pockets are especially large, double the filling recipe.

4. Place the rabbit parts in a baking dish. Top with the bacon slices. Add ¼ cup vegetable oil. Bake in the oven for 20–30 minutes, or until the rabbit is well browned. Turn once. Dribble 1 teaspoon honey over the rabbit. Season lightly with salt and pepper. Lower the oven temperature to 350°F.

5. Meanwhile, prepare the sauce by sautéing the onion and garlic in oil. Season with honey, parsley, and pepper. Add the tomatoes and wine and cook at a low boil for about 30 minutes, until the tomatoes thicken. Pour over the browned rabbit (it should be

Sauce:

1 tablespoon chopped onion
1 garlic clove, chopped
2 tablespoons vegetable oil
1 teaspoon honey
¼ teaspoon fresh parsley, chopped
⅛ teaspoon pepper
1 quart peeled tomatoes
2 tablespoons white wine
1 tablespoon butter

completely submerged in the tomatoes). Bake in the oven at 350°F. (covered) for 30–60 minutes, or until the rabbit is very tender. Add the butter to the sauce 5 minutes before serving.

boneless breast of pheasant

SERVES 4
PREPARATION TIME:
60 MINUTES

2 pheasants
1 cup breadcrumbs
1 garlic clove, finely chopped
2 tablespoons fresh parsley,
   chopped
2 tablespoons grated Parmesan
   cheese
⅓ cup flour
1 egg, well beaten with 1–2
   tablespoons water
4 tablespoons butter
4 tablespoons vegetable oil
salt and pepper to taste

Pheasant's mild flavor is almost indistinguishable from that of chicken. Be especially careful not to overcook it, however.

1. Soak the pheasants in salted water for 3–5 minutes. Rinse with cold water. Drain, then towel dry. Bone the pheasant breasts and slice. Reserve the leftover pheasant for soup.

2. Toss the bread crumbs with the garlic, parsley, and Parmesan cheese.

3. Dredge each pheasant slice in the flour, dip in the egg, and then coat with the seasoned breadcrumbs.

4. Sauté the pheasant in oil and butter over medium heat for 15–20 minutes, until tender (easily pierced with a fork). Do not overcook. Turn once. Season with salt and pepper and serve at once.

venison chops

SERVES 4
PREPARATION TIME:
45–60 MINUTES

Venison is raised commercially on game farms; however, if you know a friendly and generous hunter, perhaps he will give you some or sell it to you more cheaply. First-rate butchering, however, is essential. Venison is low in cholesterol and does not have an abundance of marbled fat; so it is important not to overcook these chops or they will become dry.

2 garlic cloves, chopped
⅓ cup chopped onion
4 ounces mushrooms, chopped
3–4 tablespoons vegetable oil
4–5 venison chops approximately
  ½-inch thick
¼ cup flour
1 egg, well beaten with 2–3
  tablespoons of water
⅓ cup breadcrumbs
salt and pepper to taste

1. Sauté the garlic, onion, and mushrooms in vegetable oil for about 5 minutes. Remove from the pan.

2. Coat the venison chops in the flour, dip them in the well-beaten egg, and then coat them with breadcrumbs. Fry over medium-high heat. Cook uncovered for 4–5 minutes on each side—less if you want rare meat. Return the mushrooms, onion, and garlic to the frying pan for about 1 minute before serving. Season with salt and pepper.

venison shoulder roast

SERVES 4–6
PREPARATION TIME:
1¾ HOURS

1 2–3-pound venison shoulder
   roast
¼ cup vegetable oil
¼–½ cup dry white wine or
   cooking sherry
¼ cup water (optional)
10–12 mushrooms, sliced
1 carrot, peeled
½ teaspoon pepper
½ teaspoon oregano
2–4 garlic cloves, chopped
½ medium-size onion, sliced
2 tablespoons fresh parsley,
   chopped
½ teaspoon rosemary
1 large bay leaf
6–8 slices uncooked bacon

Venison does not contain much marbled fat, and since roasting is cooking with dry heat, I recommend not salting this recipe until after it's cooked, as salt can draw out the juices and make it too dry.

1. Preheat the oven to 375°F.

2. Place the venison in a roasting pan. Add the oil, wine, water, mushrooms, and carrot. Sprinkle the remaining spices and flavorings over the roast. Top with the bacon slices.

3. Cover with foil and roast for 1–1½ hours (to an internal temperature of 140°–150°F.), until tender. Serve.

venison stew

SERVES 4–6
PREPARATION TIME:
2 HOURS

Neck bones and ribs are not prime cuts of venison; and so they can be chewy unless cooked slowly in liquid for a long time. This recipe turns these ordinary cuts into an enjoyable meal. Do not rush the cooking time with this cut of venison. The rule is to cook it as long as it needs to become tender.

3 pounds venison neck bones and
   ribs
¼ cup vegetable oil
1 teaspoon salt
½ teaspoon pepper
½ teaspoon oregano
1 teaspoon fresh parsley, chopped
2 bay leaves
3 garlic cloves, finely chopped
1 large onion, chopped
4 ounces mushrooms, chopped
1–1¼ cups cooking sherry
8 ounces tomato sauce

1. Remove excess fat from venison.

2. Sauté the venison in vegetable oil until browned (about 10 minutes). Season with salt, pepper, oregano, parsley, and bay leaves. Add the garlic, onion, and mushrooms. Cook over medium heat in a covered pan for 40–45 minutes or longer, until the meat is tender when pierced with a fork. Add some water if needed to prevent sticking. Stir periodically.

3. Add the cooking sherry. Cook for 20 minutes. Add the tomato sauce and enough water to cover the meat. Continue simmering (covered) until the meat falls off the bone (about 1 hour). Add more water as the liquid evaporates. Stir often. Serve hot.

elk roast and gravy

SERVES 8
PREPARATION TIME:
3 HOURS

1 7–8-pound elk roast, with the
  bone
4 garlic cloves, quartered
1 heaping tablespoon pepper
1 heaping tablespoon oregano
1 medium-size onion, sliced
7–8 slices uncooked bacon
½ cup white wine
¼ cup vegetable oil
¼ cup water
2 carrots, peeled
1 teaspoon salt
4 ounces mushrooms, chopped
2 tablespoons Worcestershire
  sauce
⅓ cup flour
2 tablespoons cold milk

I find the flavor of properly prepared elk even better than venison. If you don't tell your dinner guests what they are eating, they may believe it to be prime beef.

1. Preheat oven to 350°F.

2. Using a sharp knife, make ½-inch-deep slits in the surface of the roast and insert the garlic pieces. Place the elk in a roasting pan.

3. Sprinkle the pepper, oregano, and onion slices over the roast. Top with the bacon slices. Add the white wine, oil, water, and carrots to the pan. Cover and cook for about 2½ hours, or until tender when pierced with a fork.

4. About 15 minutes before the roast is done, pour the juices from the roast into a saucepan. Add the salt, mushrooms, and Worcestershire sauce. Simmer for 10 minutes.

5. Blend the flour and milk until all the lumps disappear. Additional water may be required to make a smooth flowing consistency.

6. Add the flour mixture slowly to the meat juices, just until the juices become thickened to the desired consistency. Stir continually as it simmers. Serve over slices of elk roast.

Seafood

"We remember the fish, which we did eat in Egypt freely; the cucumbers, and the melons, and the leeks, and the onions, and the garlick. . . ."

NUMBERS 11:5

Garlic enlivens the taste of any type of seafood: it adds zest to Shrimp Scampi and broiled scrod, enhances the taste of Clams Casino, and when combined with tomatoes and onions, makes flounder delectable.

Whatever seafood you enjoy, you are sure to find a recipe here that will suit your taste. The flounder and scrod dishes are especially good for people who enjoy fish with only a mild fishy flavor. The crab and clam recipes are a little fancier and are great for dinner parties. Most seafood lovers are familiar with the garlic-and-butter flavored Shrimp Scampi. Traditional Italian seafood dishes such as baccala and calamari are probably less familiar.

In general, fish such as cod, flounder, and pollock, contain low amounts of fat and rich amounts of highly digestible protein, plus phosphorus, potassium, and iron.

To savor its ultimate flavor, eat fish fresh. Good indicators of freshness are bright, bulging eyes; moist, shiny appearance; red gills; and no fishy odor. Fresh fish should be used as soon after purchase as possible, preferably within 24 hours. In the interim, guard against moisture loss by packaging the fish in clean plastic wrap and refrigerating it at a temperature just above freezing. When preparing fish, cook just until the translucency of its flesh disappears. Overcooked fish is dry and generally less flavorful.

Shellfish, too, tends to be lean, but in general it contains more cholesterol and slightly more sodium than fish. Shellfish should be stored at very cold temperatures and consumed soon after purchase.

baked filet of flounder

SERVES 4
PREPARATION TIME:
60 MINUTES

4 flounder filets
1–2 tablespoons vegetable oil
5–6 fresh tomatoes, peeled and
  sliced
½–¾ cup sliced onions
1–1½ tablespoons fresh parsley,
  chopped
2 garlic cloves, finely chopped
½ teaspoon oregano
½ teaspoon salt (or more, to taste)
¼ teaspoon pepper
2–3 tablespoons butter, cut into
  pieces

Flounder is a lean fish, only about 90 calories in a 4-ounce portion uncooked. The flounder family is sometimes marketed as fluke, lemon sole, and gray sole, to name a few. This method of cooking the flounder with juicy tomatoes in a covered dish is actually poaching, which keeps the fish tender and moist.

1. Preheat the oven to 350°F.

2. Rinse the filets in cold water and dry them on paper towels. Coat the inside of a baking dish with vegetable oil. Place the filets in the dish. Distribute the tomatoes and onions over the fish. Season with parsley, garlic, oregano, salt, and pepper. Distribute the butter pieces over the top.

3. Cover with foil and bake for 20–30 minutes, or until the fish is tender and no longer translucent. Serve at once.

smelts italiano

SERVES 2–4
PREPARATION TIME:
30–45 MINUTES

This small saltwater fish, a relative of the salmon, is most available from September through April. The silvery-skinned smelts average 4–6 inches in length (cleaned) and are about the size of a quarter in diameter. Choose smelts with a firm flesh and a shiny appearance. They can be boned either before or after frying.

1 pound cleaned smelts
6–8 tablespoons flour
6–8 tablespoons vegetable oil
   (enough to cover bottom of
   baking pan)
1 egg, well beaten with 1
   tablespoon water
2 cloves of garlic, chopped finely
salt and pepper to taste

1. Preheat the oven to 450°F.

2. Rinse the fish in cold water. Drain and dry on paper towels.

3. Place smelts and flour in a small plastic or paper bag. Close securely and shake to coat smelts lightly with flour.

4. Coat the bottom of a 9″ × 13″ baking dish with about ⅛″ vegetable oil. Heat the oil-coated dish in the oven until the oil is quite hot.

5. Dip the smelts in the egg and then arrange in a single layer in the baking dish. Distribute chopped garlic over the fish. Bake for ten minutes until the egg coating is golden. Serve immediately.

baked scrod in garlic butter

SERVES 3–4
PREPARATION TIME:
30–40 MINUTES

4 tablespoons butter
1 pound scrod filet
2 garlic cloves, finely chopped
2–3 tablespoons fresh parsley,
  chopped
2 tablespoons sliced onion
2 teaspoons lemon juice
salt and pepper to taste

Scrod is young codfish—very moist, with a light, delicate fish flavor.

1. Preheat the oven to 350°F.

2. Butter the bottom of a 1-inch-deep, narrow baking pan, just large enough for the filet. Place the fish in the pan and top with garlic, parsley, onion, lemon juice, and the remaining butter. Season lightly with salt and pepper.

3. Cover the pan loosely with foil and bake for 20 minutes, or until tender and no longer translucent. Serve at once.

stuffed calamari

SERVES 2
PREPARATION TIME:
60–70 MINUTES

Select small squid with bodies no longer than 6 inches, since larger ones tend to be tough. As with most seafood, cook the squid within 24 hours of purchase. Adventuresome gourmands may find the distinctive flavor and slightly spongy texture of squid especially appealing.

1 pound squid (about 8 squid)
2 tablespoons butter
1 tablespoon vegetable oil
2–3 cups tomato sauce
salt and pepper to taste

Filling:

2 eggs, beaten
¼ cup fresh parsley, chopped and packed
3 tablespoons grated Parmesan cheese
½ cup breadcrumbs
2 tablespoons chopped onion
2 garlic cloves, finely chopped
2 tablespoons milk
¼ teaspoon pepper
2 salted crackers, crumbled

1. Using your fingers, peel off and discard the purplish skin from the body and tentacles of the squid. Cut the squid body between the eyes and tentacles and discard the part of the body to which the eyes are attached. Pull out and discard the transparent quill inside the body. Soak the body and tentacles in warm salted water for 5 minutes—rinse several times. Cleaned squid should be bright white. Chop the tentacles into pieces and set aside.

2. Combine all the ingredients for the filling into a thick, moist stuffing. Fill each squid body half-full and then fasten closed with a toothpick. Allow room for expansion of the stuffing or the squid will split while cooking.

3. Sauté the stuffed squid and the chopped tentacles in butter and oil for 5–7 minutes. Then place the squid, butter and oil in a dutch oven. Cover with the tomato sauce and sprinkle with salt and pepper. Cover with a lid and simmer for 30 minutes, or until tender when pierced with a fork. Serve immediately.

clams casino

SERVES 4
PREPARATION TIME:
1 HOUR PLUS 1–2 HOURS
(OR OVERNIGHT) TO
REFRIGERATE

Hard-shelled clams are available in a variety of sizes, from small littlenecks to medium cherrystones to large quahogs, with the smallest being the most expensive. Use cherrystone clams for this recipe. Place the clams in the refrigerator for at least 1–2 hours (preferably overnight)—the cold sometimes makes them open more easily.

No salt is called for in this recipe because the combination of bacon and cheese is sufficiently salty.

20–24 cherrystone clams
½ cup breadcrumbs
2 large garlic cloves, chopped
4 teaspoons fresh parsley,
    chopped
1 teaspoon oregano
⅛ teaspoon black pepper
2 tablespoons grated locatelli (or
    Parmesan) cheese
4 tablespoons or ½ green sweet
    pepper, chopped
4–5 tablespoons butter, melted
paprika to taste
¼ pound uncooked bacon, cut
    into pieces
butter

1. Preheat the broiler.

2. Hold the clams under cold running water and scrub the shells with a vegetable brush to remove all traces of sand. Using a knife, pry open the clam shells—this may take some practice. Cut the clams out of the shell and, using utility shears, cut the clams into small pieces. Place in a colander to drain.

3. Mix the breadcrumbs, garlic, parsley, oregano, black pepper, cheese, green pepper, and melted butter. Divide the clam pieces among the 20–24 half-shells. Place 1 tablespoon of the breadcrumb mixture on top of the clams. Sprinkle paprika over it and top with the bacon pieces and butter. Broil 3–5 minutes. Turn off the heat and leave the clams in the oven for 3–5 more minutes. Serve immediately.

shrimp scampi

SERVES 2–3
PREPARATION TIME:
30 MINUTES

Shrimp are sold according to the number of shrimp per pound. A good size shrimp for scampi is 20–25 per pound. Very large shrimp tend to be tough and less flavorful. Fresh shrimp are usually marketed headless and unshelled. The flesh is almost colorless, but the shells may range in color from light brown to coral, depending on the variety or origin of the shrimp. Fresh shrimp are very perishable, so most shrimp are frozen for market. Frozen shrimp should be thawed slowly in the refrigerator just before cooking.

This dish is excellent served over rice or with pea pods.

1 pound shrimp (unshelled and
  headless)
2 large garlic cloves, finely
  chopped
2 heaping tablespoons fresh
  parsley, chopped
4 tablespoons butter
1 tablespoon vegetable oil
1–2 tablespoons dry vermouth
salt and pepper to taste
1 teaspoon flour
dash lemon juice

1. Rinse the shrimp in cold water, peel off the shells, and devein, if you wish. Dry on paper towels.

2. Sauté the garlic and parsley in butter and oil for 1–2 minutes—do not let the garlic turn brown. Add the vermouth.

3. Add the shrimp. Raise the heat to medium-high and cook for 3–5 minutes, stirring frequently. Do not overcook. Season with salt and pepper. Add 1 teaspoon flour to slightly thicken the garlic butter. Add the lemon juice during the last minute of cooking. Remove from the heat. Serve immediately.

cheesy shrimp bake

SERVES 4
PREPARATION TIME:
60–90 MINUTES

1½ pounds medium-size shrimp
   (unshelled and headless)
3 tablespoons shrimp and crab
   boil seasonings
2½–3 cups day-old Italian bread,
   cubed
4 ounces mushrooms, sliced
1 cup mozzarella cheese, grated
3 eggs
2 cups milk
1 garlic clove, finely chopped
½ teaspoon salt
½ teaspoon dry mustard
2 tablespoons fresh parsley,
   chopped
dash paprika
dash pepper

To enhance the flavor of boiled shrimp, cook them in lightly salted water seasoned with a pre-packaged blend of bay leaves, rosemary, peppercorns, red peppers, and mustard seeds called a "shrimp and crab boil."

1. Bring 1½–2 quarts lightly salted water to a boil. Add the "shrimp and crab boil" seasonings, allow to return to a boil for 3–5 minutes. Drain, then rinse in cold water. Peel and devein. Cut into bite-size pieces.

2. Preheat the oven to 350°F. Arrange half the bread cubes in a greased casserole dish. Layer the shrimp, mushrooms, and half the cheese. Then add the remaining bread cubes and cheese.

3. Beat together the eggs, milk, garlic, and remaining seasonings. Pour over the shrimp. Bake uncovered for 30–40 minutes, until the liquid is set. Serve at once.

Deveining is optional, and usually not needed for small to medium-size shrimp. However, some people find the vein to be sandy or to have an overly iodine flavor. Deveining is a simple procedure: using a sharp knife with a thin blade, trail along the dark vein, exposing the vein for easy removal.

crab casserole

SERVES 6
PREPARATION TIME:
60 MINUTES

Select only the best variety of lump back-fin crab meat. Then sort through the crab meat once or twice and discard any shells before using the crab.

1 cup milk
3 tablespoons butter
3 tablespoons flour
¼ teaspoon salt
⅛ teaspoon pepper
2 tablespoons mayonnaise
½ teaspoon dry mustard
1 teaspoon Worcestershire sauce
⅓ cup chopped onion
2 garlic cloves, finely chopped
3 tablespoons butter
2 tablespoons vegetable oil
4 ounces mushrooms, chopped
1 pound lump back-fin crab meat
1½ tablespoons fresh parsley,
    chopped
1 hard-boiled egg, chopped
    (optional)
¼ teaspoon pepper
½ teaspoon salt
⅓–½ cup breadcrumbs

1. Preheat the oven to 350°F.

2. Begin the sauce by scalding the milk in a saucepan. (Milk is scalded when small bubbles form around the sides of the pan.) Set aside. Melt 3 tablespoons butter in a skillet. Add 3 tablespoons flour, stirring quickly and constantly over low heat. Allow the butter and flour mixture to cook for 2–3 minutes, until it bubbles and thickens. Add the scalded milk ¼ cup at a time and continue to stir, working out the lumps. When the mixture is smooth and all lumps have disappeared, remove from the heat. Season with ¼ teaspoon salt and ⅛ teaspoon pepper. When the mixture has cooled, add the mayonnaise, mustard, and Worcestershire sauce and then set aside.

3. Sauté the onion and garlic in butter and vegetable oil until the onion is tender. Add the mushrooms. Sauté for 3–4 minutes longer.

4. Combine the sautéed vegetables with the crabmeat, the sauce, parsley, and chopped hard-boiled egg. Season with ¼ teaspoon pepper and ½ teaspoon salt. Pour into a greased casserole dish. Sprinkle the breadcrumbs over the top. Bake uncovered for 15 minutes, until the crab mixture begins to bubble slightly and is thoroughly heated. Serve immediately.

gram's baccala in white sauce with polenta

SERVES 4
PREPARATION TIME:
1½–2 HOURS PLUS 24–48
HOURS TO SOAK
BACCALA

Baccala is dried, salted codfish, available in Italian specialty stores. It is stiff and off-white in appearance, somewhat prehistoric looking. It must be soaked in cold water for 24–48 hours to regain some of its resiliency and to draw out the salt. Don't try to rush the soaking process, or you may end up with a dish that is too salty.

Polenta is a cornmeal staple, a substitute for bread or potatoes. It is often used to complement the distinctive flavor of baccala in white or red sauce.

1 baccala filet (about 1 pound)
1 pound cornmeal
2½–4 quarts water
3 teaspoons salt
3 cups sliced onion
1 garlic clove, chopped
4 tablespoons butter
5 tablespoons oil
1 teaspoon nutmeg
salt and pepper to taste
13 ounces evaporated milk
½–¾ cup milk

1. Cut the baccala into 2–3-inch pieces and soak it in cold water for a minimum of 24 hours. Change the water several times. The baccala is ready for cooking when it is soft and pliable. If it has not reached that stage after 24 hours, additional soaking of 12–24 hours is needed. Drain and dry on paper towels.

2. Place the cornmeal in a large pot. Slowly add 1 quart water to the cornmeal and mix until smooth. Then add 1½ quarts additional water and the salt. Bring all the ingredients to a boil, stirring constantly. Cover with a lid once it begins to boil, lower the heat to simmer, and cook for 1–1½ hours, stirring often. As the cornmeal mixture becomes thick, add boiling hot water, a little at a time (½–1 quart more water is not unusual). When it is done, polenta has a thick, smooth consistency, like cream of wheat.

3. Meanwhile sauté the onion and garlic in butter and oil for 10 minutes. Season with nutmeg, salt, and pepper. Add the baccala. Sauté (covered) until the fish breaks apart easily (about 20 minutes).

4. Add the evaporated and regular milk. Simmer for 10 minutes. Do not allow the sauce to boil or the milk may curdle. When the polenta is ready, spoon it into individual serving plates and pour the fish sauce over it. Serve immediately.

angelina's baccala and tomato stew

SERVES 2
PREPARATION TIME:
50 MINUTES PLUS 24–48
HOURS TO SOAK BACCALA

1 baccala filet (about 1 pound)
1 onion, (about 1 cup chopped)
2 bunches scallions, sliced (about
    1 cup)
2 garlic cloves, finely chopped
1 tablespoon fresh parsley,
    chopped
¼ cup raisins
1 cup celery, plus leaves, chopped
3–4 tablespoons vegetable oil
16 ounces whole, peeled toma-
    toes, mashed with a fork
2–3 medium-size potatoes, peeled
    and cut into large chunks
¾ teaspoon oregano
salt and pepper to taste

This version of baccala can be served over polenta (see Gram's Baccala and Polenta in White Sauce, page 168) or rice.

1. Cut the baccala into 3-inch pieces and soak it for at least 24 hours in cold water. Change the water several times. If the baccala is not soft and pliable after 24 hours, continue to soak it for 12–24 hours, until it reaches that stage. Drain and dry on paper towels.

2. Sauté the onion, scallions, garlic, parsley, raisins, and celery in oil for about 10 minutes.

3. Add the tomatoes and potatoes. Season with oregano and salt and pepper. Simmer (covered) until the potatoes are tender, about 25 minutes. If the sauce is too thick, add ¼–½ cup water. Add the baccala. Cover and cook until tender, 10 minutes or longer. Serve immediately.

seafood à la crème

SERVES 4
PREPARATION TIME:
60 MINUTES

½–1 cup broccoli
1 tablespoon fresh parsley,
  chopped
2 garlic cloves, chopped
3 tablespoons butter
¾–1 pound seafood chunks
1–2 teaspoons lemon juice
salt and pepper to taste
⅓–½ pound fettucini
2 tablespoons butter
¼ cup sour cream
¼ cup grated Parmesan cheese
2 tablespoons white wine
¾ cup heavy cream

"Seafood chunks" (sometimes called "sea legs") consist primarily of snow crab meat and pollock. This is a tasty, lower-cost substitute for lump back fin crab meat.

1. Steam the broccoli in a small amount of lightly salted water for about 5 minutes, until tender but not overcooked. Drain and set aside.

2. Sauté the parsley and garlic in 3 tablespoons butter for 1–2 minutes over medium heat. Do not permit the butter or garlic to turn brown. Add the seafood chunks, and allow them to heat through for about 5 minutes over medium-low heat. Add the lemon juice. Season with salt and pepper. Remove from the heat.

3. Meanwhile, cook the fettucini according to package directions, until cooked to desired doneness. Drain.

4. Prepare the cream sauce. Melt 2 tablespoons butter over low heat, add the sour cream, and stir until smooth. Blend in the grated cheese, wine, and, finally, the cream. To avoid curdling of the cream, remove the pan from the heat.

5. Combine the fettucini, broccoli, and seafood chunks. Spoon the cream sauce over all. Top with more grated cheese and serve hot.

broiled salmon with garlic sauce

SERVES 4
PREPARATION TIME:
30 MINUTES

The bright pink flesh and mild flavor of the Chinook salmon make it an ideal choice for this recipe. This native of the Pacific Northwest coast is available from April through October and is often marketed as salmon steaks, crosswise slices about 1 inch thick.

3 tablespoons butter
2 garlic cloves, minced
3 tablespoons flour (quick-mixing variety)
½ cup heavy cream
1 tablespoon cooking sherry
¼–½ cup milk
½ teaspoon lemon juice
salt and pepper to taste
4 salmon steaks (at least 1 inch thick)
salt and pepper to taste
¼ cup butter, cut in pieces

1. Preheat the broiler.

2. Melt 3 tablespoons butter in a saucepan over medium heat and sauté the garlic for 1–2 minutes. Remove the pan from the heat and add the flour, mixing well with a whisk. Return to medium heat and cook for 1–2 minutes, stirring often. Add the cream, a little at a time, continuing to whisk the sauce as it thickens. Add the sherry. Allow the sauce to simmer and then stir in ¼ cup of milk (or more, if needed) to thin the sauce to a creamy consistency (it should lightly coat a spoon). Season with lemon juice, salt, and pepper.

3. Place the salmon steaks in a greased broiling pan. Season lightly with salt and pepper. Top each piece of fish with butter. Broil for 4–5 minutes on each side. The salmon is done when the flesh is no longer translucent. Be careful not to overcook, or it will become too dry. Serve immediately, topped with the garlic sauce.

Specialties

"There is an inscription inside the pyramid which is written in Egyptian characters. It tells us of the quantity of radishes, onions, and garlic that were consumed by the workers building the pyramids. I remember most exactly that the interpreter who deciphered the inscription for me remarked that the sum of money spent on these items would amount to 1,600 talents of silver."

CONCERNING THE HISTORY OF EGYPT
Herodotus

Garlic's zestiness adds a special flavor boost to a number of snack foods and accompaniments for main dishes, several of which are featured here: Classic Garlic Bread (crispy and wonderfully garlicky), fried dough stuffed with cheeses and meats and seasoned with a hint of garlic, and pizza, with a sauce made from a delightful combination of tomatoes, onions, a whiff of anchovies, and, *la pièce de résistance*: garlic!

pizza

SERVES 6–8
PREPARATION TIME:
2¼–2½ HOURS

This recipe is for pizza fanatics who want to make the dough and sauce from scratch. Making good dough is a tricky business, but your finished product will improve with practice. The type of flour and the size of the egg vary the dough's consistency and elasticity.

For those of you with less time or patience, a frozen pizza shell or dough purchased from a bakery is easier and quicker. The sauce can be prepared ahead of time and frozen until needed.

Dough:

1 package dry yeast
¼ cup warm water
¼ teaspoon sugar
1¼ teaspoons salt
3 cups flour
1 large egg, well beaten
1 teaspoon butter, melted
¾ cup lukewarm water

Sauce:

1 small onion, chopped (about ⅓ cup)
3 garlic cloves, finely chopped
5 tablespoons vegetable oil
1–2 anchovies
1 quart peeled, crushed tomatoes

1. Dissolve the yeast in ¼ cup lukewarm water, add ¼ teaspoon sugar, and set aside for about 5 minutes (until frothy). Combine 1¼ teaspoons salt with the flour. Make a well in the center of the flour and add the well-beaten egg, the yeast mixture, and the melted butter. Add some lukewarm water a little at a time (no more than about ¾ cup in all) and mix the dough with your hands. If the dough becomes too sticky, stop adding water and sprinkle in additional flour.

2. Knead the dough on a lightly floured surface for 20 minutes, until it is smooth.

3. Shape the dough into a ball and place it in a greased bowl. Cover the bowl with a towel and place in a warm spot. Allow the dough to rise until doubled in size, about 60 minutes. Then punch down the risen dough with a floured fist. Knead for 5 minutes. Shape the dough to fit a large greased pizza tray (12″ × 17″). Cover and place in a warm spot and let rise until doubled, about 30 minutes.

1 teaspoon oregano
½ teaspoon black pepper
⅛–¼ teaspoon crushed red pepper
salt to taste (about ½ teaspoon)
pinch of sugar to taste (if
   tomatoes are sour)
vegetable oil

Topping:

⅓ cup grated Parmesan cheese
5–6 slices cheddar cheese
2 cups grated mozzarella cheese
4 ounces mushrooms, sliced

4. Prepare the pizza sauce while the dough is rising. Sauté the onion and garlic in oil for 5–7 minutes. Add the anchovies and mash them so they will dissolve. Add the mashed tomatoes. Season with oregano, black pepper, red pepper, salt, and sugar, and cook at a low boil for 15–20 minutes, until the tomatoes thicken. Cool.

5. Preheat the oven to 400°F. Spread a thin film of vegetable oil over the edges of the dough. Spoon on the pizza sauce. Bake for 20–25 minutes, until the bottom of the crust is browned. Add the cheeses and mushrooms during the last 5 minutes. Serve immediately.

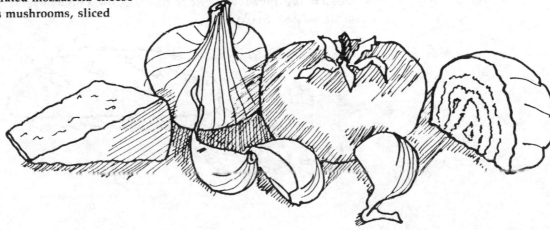

classic garlic bread

SERVES 6
PREPARATION TIME:
10 MINUTES

I have found that crusty Italian bread that is one or two days old makes the best garlic bread. You might also try day-old hoagie or steak rolls.

1 loaf day-old Italian bread (with sesame seeds)
3–4 garlic cloves, finely chopped
¼ cup butter or margarine
fresh parsley flakes (approximately 1 teaspoon)

1. Preheat the broiler.

2. Slice the bread and spread it with butter or margarine. The garlic should be chopped as finely as possible. Sprinkle it over the bread. Season lightly with the parsley.

3. Place the bread slices on heavy-duty aluminum foil and broil until the edges of the bread become golden brown. Do not take your eyes off the bread while it is broiling, or you will end up with burnt toasted. Serve hot.

savory fried dough

SERVES 4–6
PREPARATION TIME:
30 MINUTES PLUS 30
MINUTES FOR DOUGH TO
RISE

This is a quick dish for a snack or light meal. I have suggested a pepperoni-and-cheese filling, but the variety of possible fillings is as endless as your imagination. The pepperoni used in this recipe is not the 1-inch, stick-shaped, hard pepperoni, but rather a softer-textured meat, 2–3 inches in diameter, sometimes referred to as "slicing pepperoni."

You can purchase the uncooked dough from a local bakery. Usually, the dough you buy will already have risen once before being refrigerated at the bakery. So it will need to rise once more.

1 loaf uncooked Italian bread
   dough
1 garlic clove, finely chopped
¼ pound pepperoni, sliced
½ pound muenster cheese, sliced
½ cup vegetable oil

1. Place the dough in a large greased bowl, cover it with waxed paper, and place it in a warm spot until the dough doubles in bulk (about ½ hour).

2. Tear the dough into pieces and press it into approximately 16 flat, round shapes, about 3 inches in diameter. Distribute the finely chopped garlic over the pieces of dough. Place slices of pepperoni and cheese on top of the dough. Fold the dough over the filling, and press the edges to seal the dough together, being careful not to tear the dough.

3. Heat the vegetable oil in a large skillet. When it is hot, add the dough pockets. The dough will puff up as it cooks. Cook until golden brown (5–7 minutes). Drain on paper towels and serve immediately.

bagno caldo

The name of this Northern Italian dish literally means "hot bath." It is a garlic-laden, anchovy-based sauce that is served hot as a dip for crisp vegetables or crusty Italian bread. There are two versions presented here. The first is a rich, creamy sauce. The second, a lighter sauce, omits the cream but uses more olive oil.

bagno caldo with cream

YIELD: 1¼–1½ CUPS
PREPARATION TIME:
30 MINUTES

2 ounces canned anchovies
   (packed in oil)
3 garlic cloves, finely chopped
2 tablespoons vegetable or olive
   oil
½ cup butter
1 cup heavy cream

1. Heat the anchovies and the oil in which they are packed in a saucepan over medium heat. Mash with a fork while cooking until the anchovies dissolve.

2. Add the garlic, oil and butter and simmer on low heat, allowing the garlic to flavor the sauce. Remove from heat.

3. In a separate pan, bring the cream to a boil, stirring continually for about 15 minutes until the cream thickens slightly.

4. Re-heat the anchovy mixture and add the cream gradually, stirring to combine into a smooth sauce.

5. The sauce must remain warm while being served, so place it in a chafing dish at the table. Have a platter of crisp, chilled vegetables such as carrot and celery sticks and pepper slices and an assortment of bread sticks and slices of crusty French or Italian bread for dipping in the sauce.

bagno caldo with olive oil

YIELD: ¾–1 CUP
PREPARATION TIME:
15 MINUTES

2 ounces canned anchovies
   (packed in oil)
6 tablespoons olive oil
½ cup butter
3 garlic cloves, finely chopped
1 teaspoon fresh parsley, chopped

1. Place the anchovies and the oil in which they were packed in a skillet and cook over medium heat until the anchovies dissolve. Add the olive oil, butter and the garlic and sauté on low for 1–3 minutes. Season with parsley.

2. Serve while keeping dish warm over a tabletop heating element. Have on hand chunks of crusty bread, breadsticks, and slices of celery, carrots and green peppers for dipping in the sauce. You may like to try cutting up the vegetables and adding them to the sauce for 1–2 minutes prior to removing the sauce from the burner.

aïoli

YIELD: 1 CUP
PREPARATION TIME:
30 MINUTES

This garlic-flavored mayonnaise is sometimes referred to as the "butter of Provence," named for the region of France where it originated. It is served as an accompaniment to cold meats or vegetables. French cooks often add it to fish stock to create a soup called "bourride."

Variations of this basic recipe include a Greek version called "skordalia" with chopped parsley, pulverized almonds and finely ground fresh breadcrumbs. Skordalia may be served over hard-boiled eggs or boiled potatoes.

4 garlic cloves, finely chopped
2 tablespoons breadcrumbs
1–2 teaspoons vinegar
4 egg yolks (room temperature)
1 cup vegetable oil or olive oil
dash of ground mustard
½ teaspoon lemon juice (optional)
¼ teaspoon salt
2–4 teaspoons boiling water

1. In a small bowl, mash the chopped garlic into a smooth paste using the back of a wooden spoon.

2. In a separate bowl, moisten the breadcrumbs with vinegar so that crumbs will stick together when pressed. Add to the mashed garlic.

3. Add the egg yolks one at a time to the garlic and breadcrumbs, mixing well until a thick paste is formed.

4. Using an egg beater, add the oil ½ teaspoon at a time, beating between additions. After ½ cup has been added, the oil can be added somewhat faster, 1 teaspoon at a time.

5. Season with the mustard, lemon juice (optional) and salt.

6. Add 2–4 teaspoons boiling water, one teaspoon at a time, mixing well until desired consistency is attained. The mixture may be refrigerated for a few days. If the oil separates, beat with a whisk to recombine.

hummus

YIELD: 1 CUP
PREPARATION TIME:
10 MINUTES

1 cup chick peas, cooked
1 large garlic clove, finely chopped
¼ cup tahini
¼ teaspoon salt
½ teaspoon vinegar
3 tablespoons vegetable oil
4 tablespoons water

This Middle Eastern dip or spread is made with chick peas (also known as garbanzo beans) seasoned with zesty garlic, and tahini, a thick sesame paste.

In a blender, mash the chick peas and the garlic into a thick paste. In a separate bowl, combine the tahini with the salt, vinegar, 2 tablespoons oil and 1 tablespoon water and mix well. Add this tahini mixture to the blender. Blend with the remaining oil and water until smooth. Add more water or oil as needed to obtain desired consistency. Serve as a dip for cracker or matzoh.

roasted garlic

YIELD: ¼ CUP, ENOUGH
FOR 4–8 SLICES OF BREAD
PREPARATION TIME:
35 MINUTES

1 bulb of garlic
1 tablespoon fresh parsley, chopped
2 tablespoons vegetable oil
3 tablespoons butter

This is great as a spread for crusty Italian bread, which soaks up the butter, or on crackers.

Preheat the oven to 350°F. Separate the bulb of garlic into individual cloves. Peel and place in a small baking dish. Add the parsley, oil and butter. Cover and bake for about 30 minutes, until soft. Mash with a fork and spread on crusty Italian bread.

Index

Garlic butter, 10
  with ravioli, 89
  with scrod, 162
Garlic oil, 10
Garlic-flavored vinegar, 10
Garlicky roast chicken, 138
Gazpacho soup, 5, 75
Glorious garlic soup, 56
Gnocchi, 80, 85
Gram's baccala in white sauce with polenta, 168–169
Gravy, brown, 127
Gray sole, 160
Greece, use of garlic, 6, 8, 124–125, 182
Green peppers, Szechuan-style beef and, 131

H

Hearty bean soup, 64–65
Hecate, 8
Henry IV, 8
Herodotus, 174
Hippocrates, 6
Hummus, 5, 183
Hunan cuisine, 5. *See also* Oriental dishes

I

India, medical use of garlic, 7
Israeli cuisine, 5
Israelites, use of garlic, 7
Italian cuisine, 4, 159
Italian long-neck squash
  soup, 60
  stuffed, 103, 110–111
Italian plum tomatoes, 30, 82, 84, 105
Italian sausage, 147
Italy, use of garlic, 8

J

Japanese vermicelli, 80

K

Kale *au gratin*, 23
Korean beef and vegetables, 130
Korean vermicelli, 130

L

Lamb, 115, 116, 124
  moussaka, 124–125
  roast leg of, 125
Lasagna, 80, 89
Lemon and herb chicken, 136
Lemon sole, 160
Lentil soup, 55, 62
Lima beans, veal and, 122
Linguine, 79
  pesto, 95
Locatelli, 90
Long-neck squash. *See* Italian long-neck squash

M

Macaroni salad, 49
Mafalde, 79
Mandarin chicken for two, 142
Manicotti, 80, 91
Marinades, 115, 133
Maureen's tomato sauce, 84
Mayonnaise, 5, 182
Meat, 115–117. *See also* specific kinds
  aging of, 115
  fat, 115, 117
  grades, 115
  tenderness, 115
Meat loaf, 134
Meatballs, 83
  for soup, 67
Middle-Eastern cuisine, 5, 183
Min's baked cream of squash, 35
Mohammed, 6
Mom's tomato sauce and meatballs, 82–83
Mortadella, 123
Moussaka, 124–125
Mozzarella, 88
Mushrooms, 44
  stuffed, 44
  velvet soup, 55, 69
  wild, 45

N

Nereids, 8
1985 Jersey Fresh Festival, 17
Numbers 11:5, 158

O

Odysseus, 8
Oil, amount for frying, 14
Oriental dishes
  Cantonese beef with snow peas, 132
  Korean beef and vegetables, 130
  mandarin chicken for two, 141
  Oriental chicken wings, 143
  Szechuan-style beef and green peppers, 131

P

Parmesan, 90
  eggplant, 104
  potato fritters, 47
Pasta, 79–81
  angel hair, 139
  cauliflower and, 97
  clams and spaghetti, 98
  cooking of, 80–81
  crabs and spaghetti, 99
  gnocchi, 80, 85
  homemade, 80
  lasagna, 88–89
  macaroni salad, 49
  manicotti, 91
  Oriental vermicelli, 80, 130
  pasta and beef soup, 63
  pasta e fagioli, 55, 74
  pasta with tuna sauce, 100
  pesto linguine, 95
  ravioli della nonna braida, 86–87
  ravioli with garlic butter, 89
  in soups, 55, 63, 73, 80
  spinach fettucini royale, 94
  stuffed shells, 80, 90
  tortellini, 73, 79, 80, 92–93
  varieties of, 79–80
  zucchini and, 96
Pasteur, Louis, 6
Peas, chick, 50, 183
Peas, snow, with Cantonese beef, 132
Pepperoni, 179
Peppers, 42, 107
  antipasto with potatoes, peppers, and tomatoes, 30
  "bullnose," 108
  pickled, 42
  and sausage Napolitano, 147